Film Actresses

Volume 15

Claudette Colbert

Documentary study

Part 1

ISBN-13 : 978-1502930811

ISBN-10 : 1502930811

Dtp
and
graphic design

Iacob Adrian

Author statement

The actors and actresses are the the bricks .

The cast and crew are the plaster .

They stand on the foundation created by
producers and writers and directors .

All these people creates the great palace
of the art of film .

Iacob Adrian - 2013

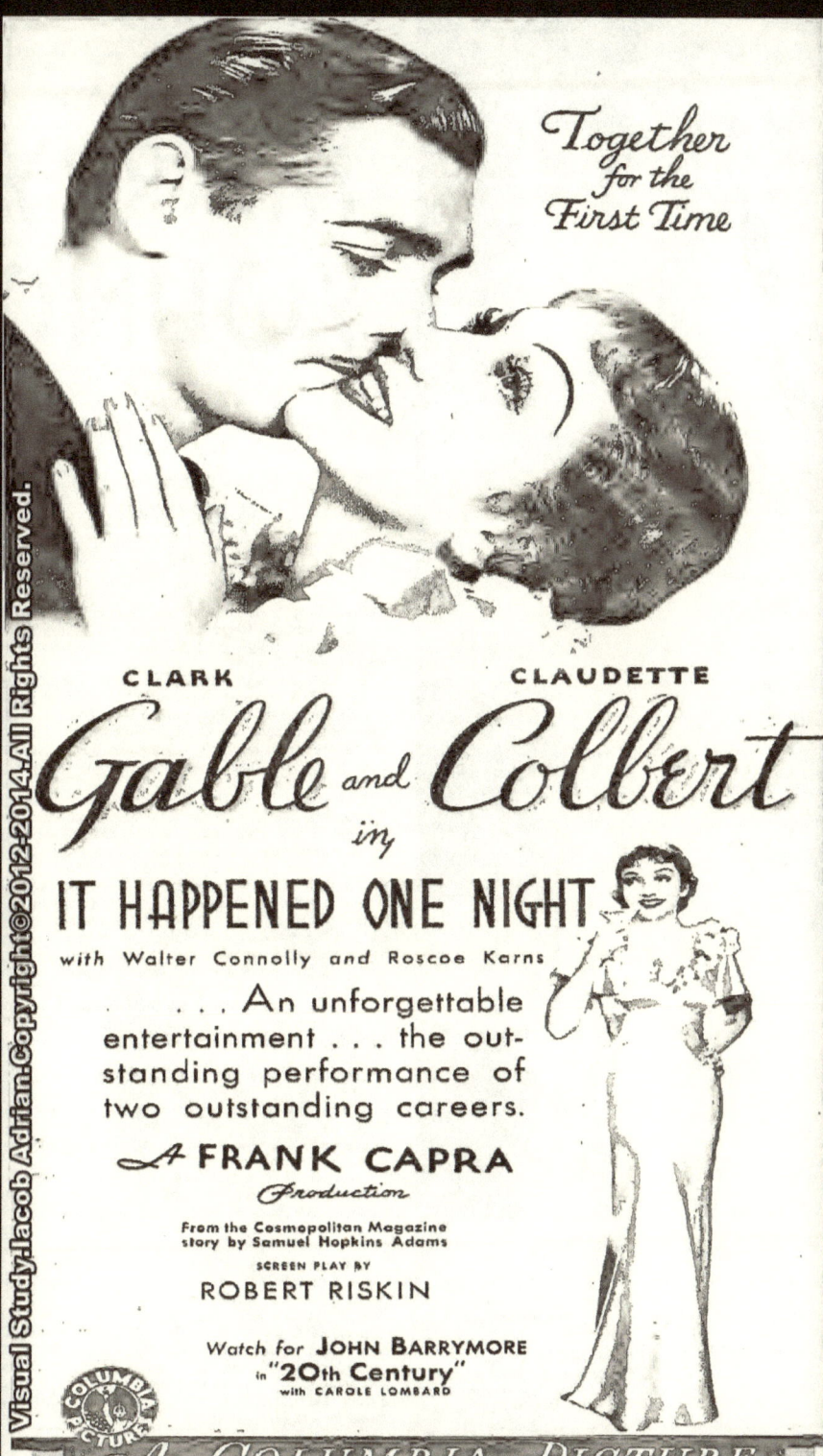

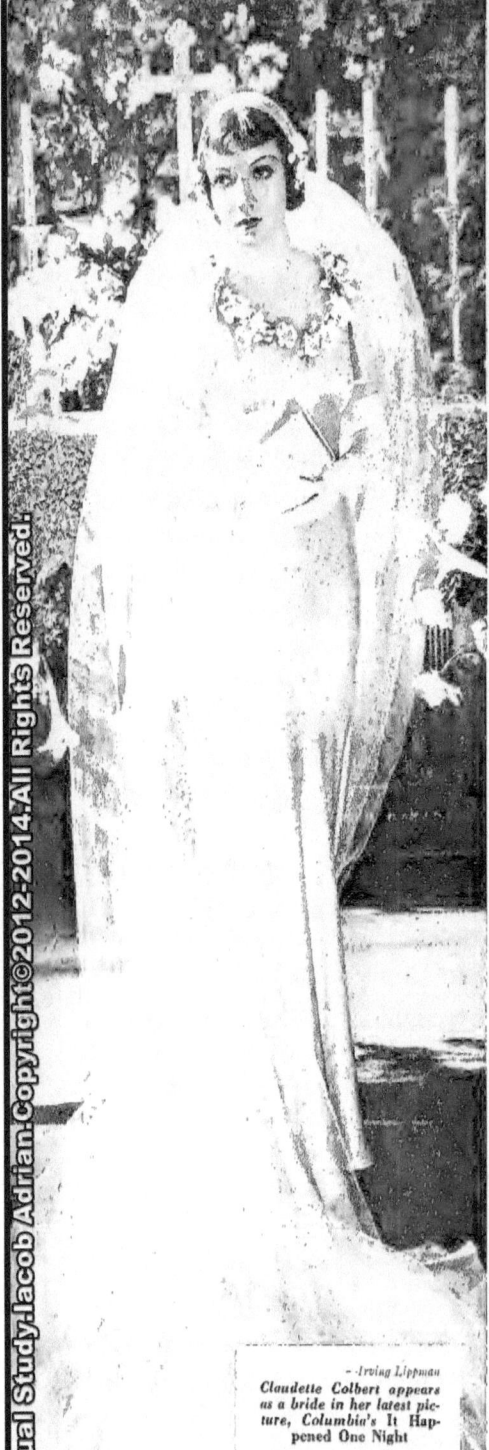

- Irving Lippman
Claudette Colbert appears as a bride in her latest picture, Columbia's It Happened One Night

CLAUDETTE COLBERT SAYS

MARRY YOUNG

Claudette Colbert gives a convincing argument in favor of early marriage

by JERRY LANE

TAKE LOVE WHEN you find it! That is Claudette Colbert's advice. Claudette, who has the French flair for living life fully—and the French appreciation of the art of love.

"It's the most tragic thing in the world," she told me as we sat in the living room of her hillside home, "the number of girls who are deliberately putting love out of their lives. Some of them have been caught in an economic whirlpool. Others are afraid marriage will hamper them. Yet marriage is the one thing every woman needs to make her complete,

"I tell you quite frankly I don't think anything can equal the supreme joy of young love. Nothing can make up to two people who really love and understand one another for wasted years—those long years of loneliness.

● "On the boat coming back from Honolulu recently I met a girl by the name of Stephanie, a traveling companion for an old lady. Stephanie told me about herself and her Tommy—how they couldn't marry because Tommy has a mother to support and two small sisters to put through school, while she must care for a paralytic father and an aunt on a meager salary.

"There they were, two young things trying to stave off the greatest force in life. Trying to forget what might have been if they hadn't been caught in a hopeless web of circumstance.

"*And the terrible part of it is that there are a million Stephanies and Tommies in the world right now!*" Claudette watched the vivid sunset for a long moment. Then she chuckled softly. "You know what I told Stephanie? I told her to see Tommy the minute the boat landed and find a preacher.

"You see, there's usually a way of fooling fate. Of taking it in your own two hands and twisting it to your needs." She chuckled again. And this Colbert girl has the most irresistible, confiding chuckle in the world. "That's exactly what Norman Foster and I did!

"We were nothing but kids when we went down to the city hall for a license. Kids with plenty of obligations, too. Norman had his people to look after and I had mine. Neither of us had any money—no one gets paid during rehearsals—and we were married the morning after *The Barker* opened. Our parts in that play were the first breaks for both of us. We hadn't the faintest idea of how long it was going to run. Actors never do. 'Tomorrow' is always a desperate chance with them. You may get a big salary

Please turn to page sixty-four

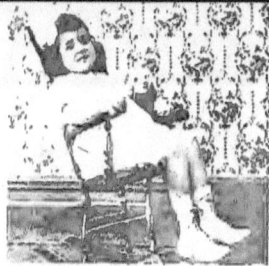

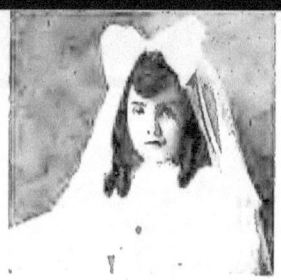

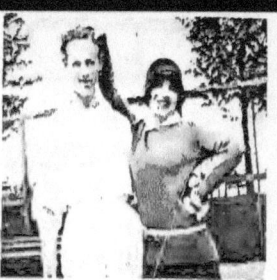

Claudette Colbert at the age of three listening to her Grandpa sing in Paris. When she was six her parents moved to the United States

When Claudette was eight years of age she received her first communion in New York. She lived in the heart of Manhattan

Leslie Howard and Claudette became close friends when she was appearing on the Chicago stage in 1926 and often played tennis together

STEPPING STONES

THE GLAMOROUS TRUE LIFE STORY OF CLAUDETTE COLBERT

Claudette's latest film is It Happened One Night in which Columbia stars her with Clark Gable

THERE WAS NO doubt about it; Grandpa could sing.

Not good, perhaps, but loud. Very loud. So loud that his powerful voice shook the living room of the little farmhouse so that four-year-old Claudette Chauchoin listened in fear lest the white-washed ceiling should tumble in upon her.

Claudette Chauchoin, Claudette Colbert to be, recalls the scene in the farmhouse as one of her first recollections. It is stamped deep in her memory, as these early childhood impressions usually are. Since those days, many things have happened to Claudette. She has become a star on both stage and screen, met success and failure, had the thrill of great personal success—but she still counts the sight of her tall, white-haired grandparent singing in the low-ceiled room, one of the most impressive of her life.

Grandpere Chauchoin had been educated for an operatic career in his youth, but his dream of becoming an opera star never matured. After marriage he settled down to the more certain and profitable one of a French farmer. Grandpa sang with a voice far more powerful than musical, but to the little Claudette it was one of the most wonderful voices in the world.

The future film star was born in Paris in 1907, in the section, just within the walls, called Sainte Mandé. She remembers little of her early life in Paris except the long walks with her mother in the Bois de Boulogne which was very near her home. Sometimes it was her elder brother, Charles, who took her on these walks. On Sunday afternoons it was her father, Georges.

Papa Georges and Mama Jeanne had many things to talk about while Claudette and brother Charles were on their strolls in the park. Georges, never too successful as a business man, had met with two reverses in a row.

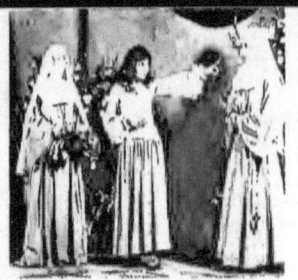

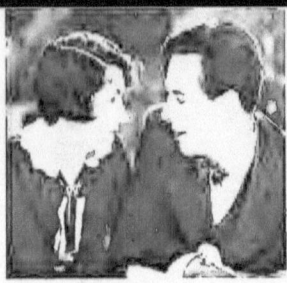

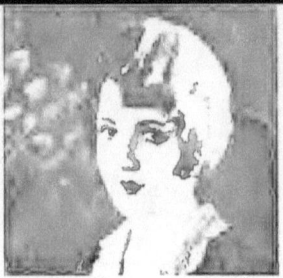

Claudette (center) and two members of the cast of La Gringa, the first play in which she starred on the stage. That was in 1928

Claudette and Ben Lyon were featured in For the Love of Mike, her first movie which was filmed in 1927 under Frank Capra's direction

Claudette's first big stage chance came when she appeared with the Leah Kleschna Co. in Chicago during the first year of her career

TO FAME

by CLARK WARREN

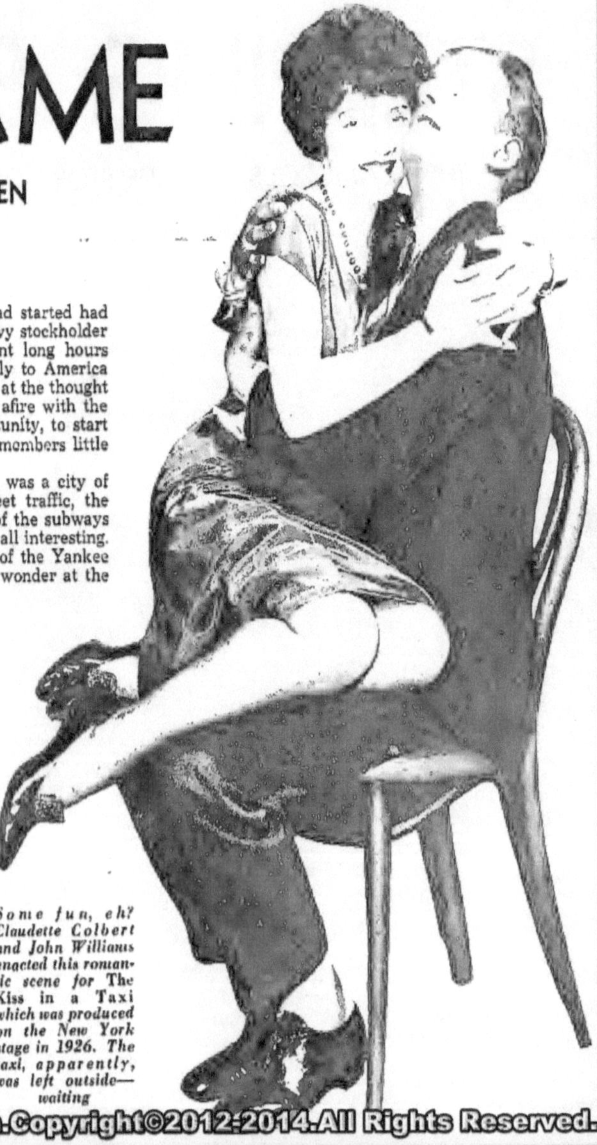

A chain of pastry and bon-bon shops he had started had failed; an ink factory in which he was a heavy stockholder had gone to the wall, and the couple spent long hours debating the advisability of taking the family to America and starting anew. Mama Jeanne cried often at the thought of leaving her dear Paris, but Georges was afire with the desire to get to America, the land of opportunity, to start again in that land of promise. Claudette remembers little of the trip to America.

New York, to a six-year-old French girl, was a city of wonders. The roar and bustle of the street traffic, the screech of elevated trains, and the rumble of the subways were sometimes terrifying to her, but it was all interesting. She could not speak or understand a word of the Yankee language, but she could stare in open-eyed wonder at the hurrying crowds, the huge buildings and all the strange, new sights which greeted her eyes at every turn.

Papa Georges soon ensconced his family in an apartment in Fifty-third street at Lexington Avenue and set out to look for a position. His letters of introduction finally won him a post in the foreign department of the First National bank.

● Claudette can not remember when she first learned to speak English. It was not at home, where neither of her parents spoke it. All family conversations were in her native tongue. Even when her mother and father could speak English, they insisted that Claudette and Charles address them in French.

"It wasn't because they didn't like America or the English language," explains Claudette. "Mother knew she spoke with an accent, and knew that I would retain my own accent if she talked to me in broken French-English. She preferred that I learn it at school, from my teachers."

Some fun, eh? Claudette Colbert and John Williams enacted this romantic scene for The Kiss in a Taxi which was produced on the New York stage in 1926. The taxi, apparently, was left outside—waiting

Stepping Stones to Fame

Of her early school days she remembers vividly that she was always called upon to sing little solos, and to speak pieces before the class more often, she says, than any other pupil. Claudette modestly claims it was because of her accent which the teacher and the class found amusing.

From the grammar school she entered Washington Irving high school and for the first time in her life was allowed to enter into social and class activities. She made the basketball team and was asked to join the French dramatic club, because she could speak the language. In the few plays in which she appeared, she attracted the attention of her English teacher, Alice Rostetter, who drafted her into the English dramatic club.

Miss Rostetter took a deep interest in her little pupil, as she believed the girl had talent which should be developed. She was acquainted with several of the Provincetown players in Greenwich Village, and had sold the organization several plays and playlets. The theatre was located on McDougal street, in the very heart of the Village.

The teacher persuaded Jasper Deeter, manager of the troupe, to give her protegé a chance, and soon Claudette was rehearsing for *The Widow's Veil*.

HIGH SCHOOL graduation day came, and Claudette sallied forth to face the world, secure in the thought that the studies of art and designing, which she had mastered in her high school classes, would fit her to battle for a livelihood. Father Georges was still in the bank, and promotion was not as rapid as his enthusiastic fervor in France had imagined.

With a pad of sketches under her arm, Claudette went into the world in search of a position as designer. From one store to another she carried the bulky bundle. At last, one store manager informed her that he had a job for her in the workrooms and Claudette accepted it.

It was not a bit like the little would-be artist imagined, for she was little better than a janitor than a designer, carrying heavy bundles of materials, and ceaselessly struggling to keep the floor swept clean of scraps of material. In vain she appealed to the manager to allow her to design a few gowns and she was met with the usual refusal until one day, when the other artists were overbusy, he asked her to turn in a half-dozen designs for blouses.

Claudette worked all morning on her first sketch. In her ignorance she tried to make it a full drawing. "A regular portrait it was," she says, and had hardly got a start on the design before the manager asked her for her sketches. Claudette showed him the half-completed work of art.

"Where are the other five?" the manager asked.

"The other five—this is all there is—" Claudette gasped.

That ended her career in that shop then and there.

Seeing that the future in art was somewhat nebulous, Claudette found a few pupils to whom she taught French, dabbling in art in her spare time.

It was the French lessons which led her back to the theatre. Among her small list of pupils was Helen Hackett,

an actress, who told her again that she should go on the stage. She introduced Claudette to Ann Morrison, who was about to produce *The Wild Westcotts* on Broadway. Miss Morrison gave the girl a chance.

Claudette's big Broadway debut consisted of a rôle as one of three guests at a house party—and her speeches were three lines. But she got a thrill out of it. First presentation of the play was at the Frazee Theatre, on Christmas 1924.

HARDLY HAD *The Wild Westcotts* closed before Claudette was sitting in Brock Pemberton's office telling him what a great actress she was. Pemberton had never heard of the dark-haired and dark-eyed miss, which was a good thing for Claudette, for she told him a string of white lies. She told him of the hundreds of plays in which she had appeared in France; of a theatrical ancestry which dated back to Charlemagne. It was sufficiently impressive, for Pemberton gave her a leading rôle in *The Marionette Man*, which starred Ulric Haupt, the great German player.

She fooled Pemberton—but she couldn't fool Haupt.

"He knew I was faking the first scene we had together," says Claudette. "He was a good sport, though, and didn't betray me."

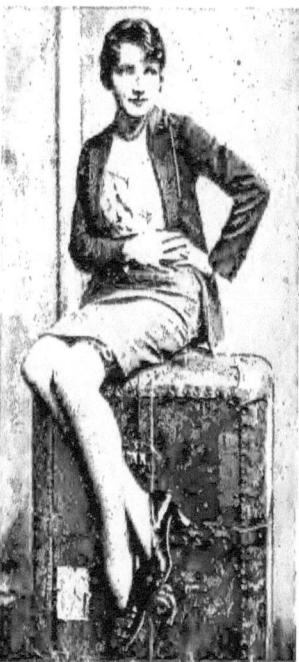

Claudette Colbert as she appeared in The Barker on Broadway in 1927. She met her future husband, Norman Foster, while playing in this production. It was her last stage rôle before entering pictures

It was at this time that Claudette decided to drop the family name "Chauchoin" and adopt that of her grandmother. She called herself Claudette Colbert, and pronounced it to rhyme with "shirt." It is only since she entered motion pictures that she has been pronouncing the name to rhyme with "care."

But although Claudette had picked the stage as her life work, Papa and Mamma Chauchoin had other ideas. The stage, to them, was a place only for bad and fallen women and decidedly not the place for a French girl of tender up-bringing. It was not for a long time that the parental scowl was missing every time the theatre was mentioned.

Claudette's mother was won over first. Her father, up to the time of his death, would never openly admit that he was proud of his daughter. But, although he would not say so, he was secretly proud of his daughter and of her success.

"A few days before my first starring rôle in *The Kiss in the Taxi* he passed on.

When *The Marionette Man* closed, Claudette Colbert determined to get more training and turned to stock companies, the school of experience that has turned out so many fine players.

Among those to whom she applied was Jesse Bonstell, and Claudette being very, very eager to work, made enough of an impression to bring a query from the producer as to what salary she expected.

"I had heard that stock players were obliged to purchase their own wardrobe," says Claudette, "so I spoke right up and asked for $200 a week. I have never heard anyone laugh harder nor longer than Miss Bonstell when she heard my request. It was nearly five minutes before she recovered enough breath to explain to me that stock players were usually paid thirty-five or forty dollars a week, and to ask wherever I had got the impression that salaries ran that high. She was very nice about it, though, and explained that she couldn't use me just then.

"In less than two weeks, though, she called me on the telephone. Katherine Alexander was leaving the cast of *Leah Kleschna*—and she could use me in Miss Alexander's rôle. I hustled right down to the office and signed."

Then followed ten weeks in such a fine company! Arnold Daly! William Faversham! Lowell Sherman! Helen Gahagen! Jose Rubin—and Claudette Colbert!

The play went to Chicago and finished its run there. It was during the Chicago engagement that she met Leslie Howard who gave her a letter to Al Woods, the New York theatrical producer.

BACK IN New York, she presented her letter to Al Woods, who was properly impressed with the fact that she had been one of the illustrious *Leah Kleschna* troupe. He gave her a rôle in a new play, *The Cat Came Back*, which opened in Chicago. It died aborning there, and never lived to see the lights of Broadway.

Although *The Cat Came Back* had only a short run, it was enough to impress Woods with Claudette's ability, and he gave her the leading feminine rôle in *A Kiss in a Taxi*. It survived a Chicago engagement and moved to New York, and Claudette Colbert's name blazed from the marquee lights as leading lady. She was such a success that the wiley Woods lost

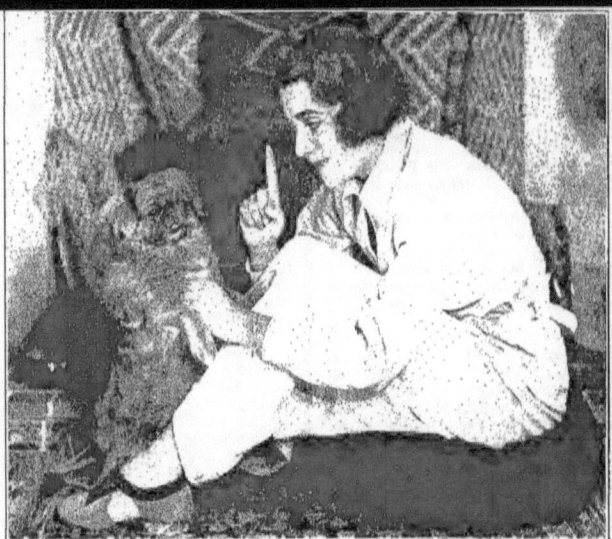

Ruby Keeler devotes some of her spare time after filming Dames for Warner Brothers to teaching her Peke some new tricks. She was snapped before the fireplace of the home at Burbank which she shares with her husband, Al Jolson

no time in signing her to a five-year contract.

Between his own shows and farming her out to other producers, Woods kept Claudette very busy. She played in rapid succession in *Tin Pan Alley, High Stakes, Fast Life, La Gringa, The Mulberry Bush, The Ghost Train, Pearl of Great Price,* and *Dynamo,* her fame and ability mounting with every performance.

War broke out anew between them shortly after when Woods wanted her to do the leading rôle in his new play, *Crime.* Claudette wanted to do a play for the Selwyns, called *The Barker.* She had read the manuscript and loved the play, and did not care for the part in *Crime.* She told Woods that it wasn't a good part for her.

"You're crazy," he shouted. "It's a great part—a regular star-making part. Go with the Selwyns; I'll take an unknown girl, put her in *Crime* and make her famous!"

Woods found his unknown, put her in the rôle. She was a sensation. The girl was Sylvia Sidney. Claudette wasn't wrong, though, about the merits of the rôle in *The Barker.* It did as much for her as *Crime* did for Sylvia Sidney.

IT Not Only firmly established her as a star, but it introduced her to the man destined to be her future husband, Norman Foster, the juvenile in the production.

"The first time I saw Norman I was disappointed," Claudette declares. "It was at the first day of rehearsals. I asked Walter Huston, who had the featured rôle, which of the players was the juvenile. Naturally, I was interested, for most of my scenes were with him. Walter pointed to a man, sitting on the stage floor, on a telephone book. I was disappointed for he seemed only about three feet tall. It wasn't until he stood up that I realized that he was quite a man."

Almost exactly three weeks to a day after that first meeting, Claudette and Norman were engaged.

"We did keep it from the public, though, and from my mother. She would never have approved of an actor as a husband, as has been reported. We didn't have time. Mother didn't discover we were married until a year later, when she read it in Walter Winchell's column."

WHEN CLAUDETTE came back from the London run of the play, she was offered contracts in motion pictures, which she steadfastly refused. She had made one silent picture during her contract with Woods, and didn't like them at all. But about this time, talking pictures became possible, and Claudette's interest in the screen was awakened.

By a strange co-incidence, the silent picture, *For The Love of Mike* was directed by a young man by the name of Frank Capra. It was quickly and cheaply made, and one of the first feature length productions Capra had ever directed. Her latest picture, and one in which she has established herself as one of the great stars of the screen, *It Happened One Night,* in which she is costarred with Clark Gable, was also directed by Frank Capra, now one of the screen's greatest directors. Ben Lyon also played in *For The Love of Mike.*

Motion picture offers that required her to go to California were consistently refused by Claudette. She didn't want to be separated from Norman, her husband.

Then Paramount offered her a contract and she refused it. She would not go to California. They told her that she didn't have to cross the continent; all she had to do was to cross the bridge into Long Island city, and so she signed and Woods sold his contract with her to the motion picture concern.

The arrangement of separate living quarters for Claudette and Norman, which startled Hollywood and caused

much speculation, wasn't intentional. Neither of them anticipated such a thing. When they went to London together in *The Barker,* they had dreamed of a husband-and-wife team that would grow to everlasting fame together.

But it wasn't to be. Claudette received her offer from Paramount and the contract which followed. Norman, too, had received many screen offers and finally signed with Paramount just to be near his wife, with the idea in mind that they could be as famous as a husband-and-wife screen team as they could be on the stage. That they wouldn't be featured together, or that they might even be separated by some three thousand miles never occurred to them. But that's just what happened.

Paramount sent Norman to California and Claudette was kept in New York.

Foster made his picture in Hollywood and then calmly told B. P. Schulberg, production head, that he was going to New York to visit his wife. Schulberg just as cooly told Norman that he was going to start him in a picture on the next day.

"That didn't appeal to Norman at all," says Claudette. "Norman was stymied until he told his troubles to a lawyer friend who dug up an old California law that provided that no employer could keep husband and wife apart more than three months.

"Armed with a copy of the law, Norman went to Mr. Schulberg. Seeing nothing he could do but bow gracefully to the situation, Schulberg gave him the permission and Norman took the train the next day."

Paramount got smart. They sent Claudette to California.

But by this time, Claudette and Norman were accustomed to living apart. When they met again it was like a new honeymoon and so they decided to maintain separate establishments, retain their own hours, their own careers, and their own privacy. Claudette sent for her mother and her aunt, took a house, and settled down. Norman rented a place just a short walk away. It worked out wonderfully well.

WHEN CLAUDETTE first came to Hollywood, she hated the place.

"I loved New York so much that I couldn't get interested in any other city," she declares. "But I've gotten over that. Today I'm living in the first house I've ever occupied, and I've got my own garden and my own flowers—and it's grand! Would I go back to New York? Ye-e-e es —I might—but I'm not eager to go—right now.

Claudette's present home is in Brentwood, one of the most beautiful sections of Los Angeles. It is the house previously occupied by Greta Garbo.

Claudette finds many things about California that she likes, and doesn't hesitate to tell which she likes and which she doesn't. The beaches, which so many easterners find so attractive, do not appeal to her. She isn't crazy about bathing. She loves to motor and often takes long drives in the evening after the day's work at the studio is finished.

And she likes to play golf, although she admits that her game is bad. Tennis is her favorite sport.

Most of her friends are not in motion picture circles. However, she numbers the two movie Joans, Crawford and Blondell, among her intimates, and also Mrs. Paul Lukas and Mrs. Samuel Goldwyn.

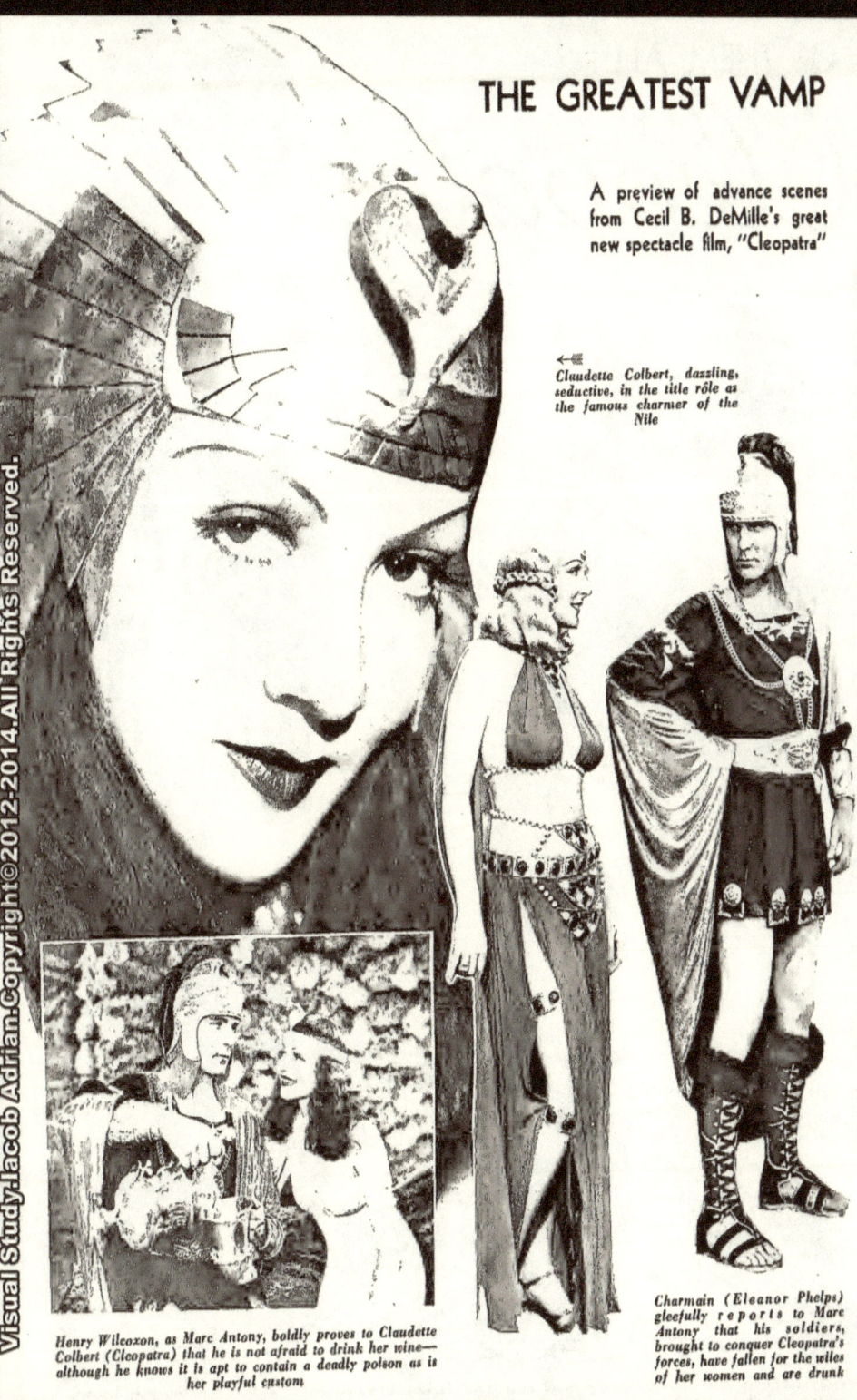

THE GREATEST VAMP

A preview of advance scenes from Cecil B. DeMille's great new spectacle film, "Cleopatra"

Claudette Colbert, dazzling, seductive, in the title rôle as the famous charmer of the Nile

Henry Wilcoxon, as Marc Antony, boldly proves to Claudette Colbert (Cleopatra) that he is not afraid to drink her wine—although he knows it is apt to contain a deadly poison as is her playful custom.

Charmain (Eleanor Phelps) gleefully reports to Marc Antony that his soldiers, brought to conquer Cleopatra's forces, have fallen for the wiles of her women and are drunk

OF THEM ALL!
Cleopatra

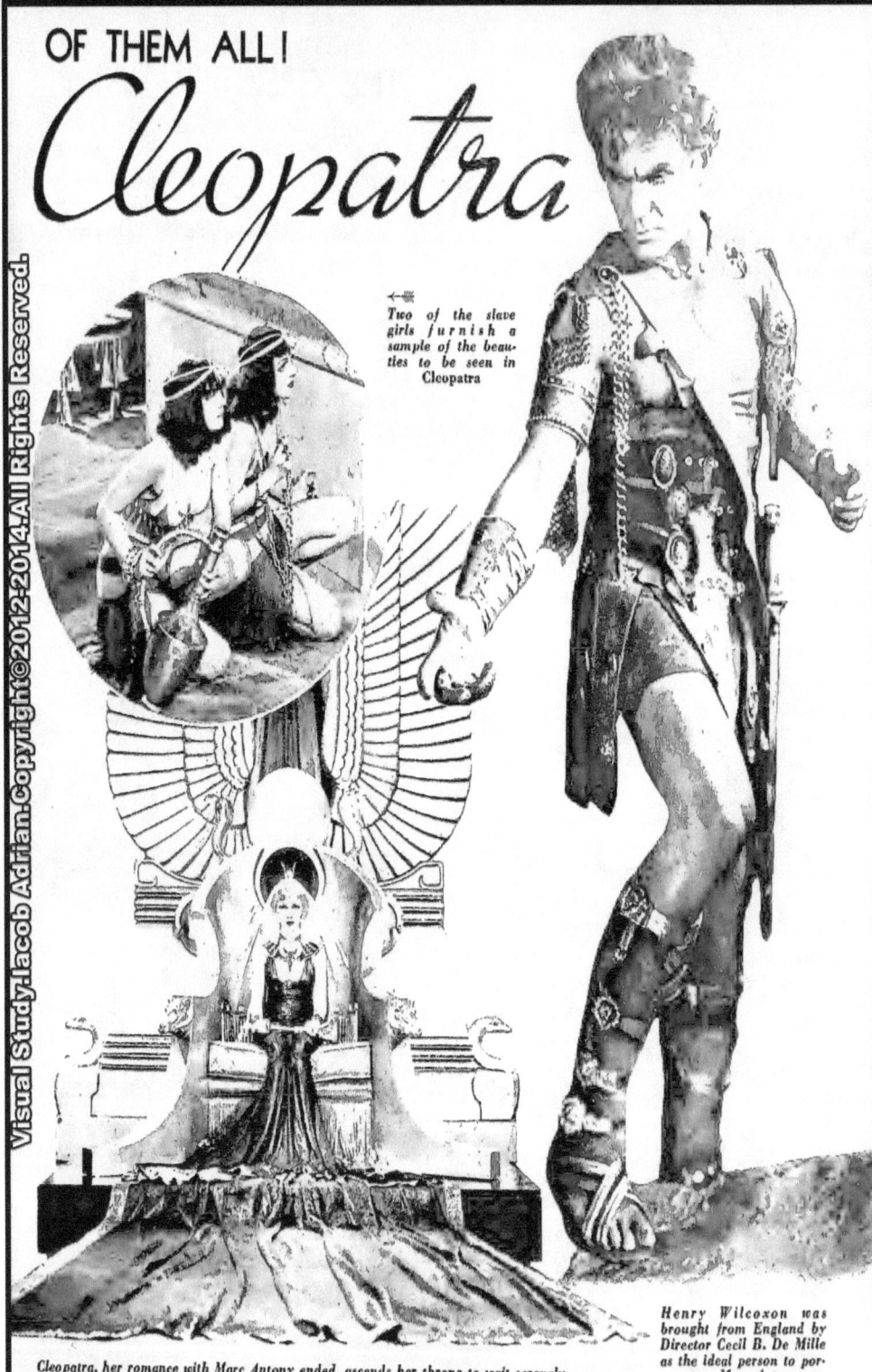

Two of the slave girls furnish a sample of the beauties to be seen in Cleopatra

Cleopatra, her romance with Marc Antony ended, ascends her throne to wait serenely for the death that is certain to come as the result of permitting an asp to bite her

Henry Wilcoxon was brought from England by Director Cecil B. De Mille as the ideal person to portray Marc Antony

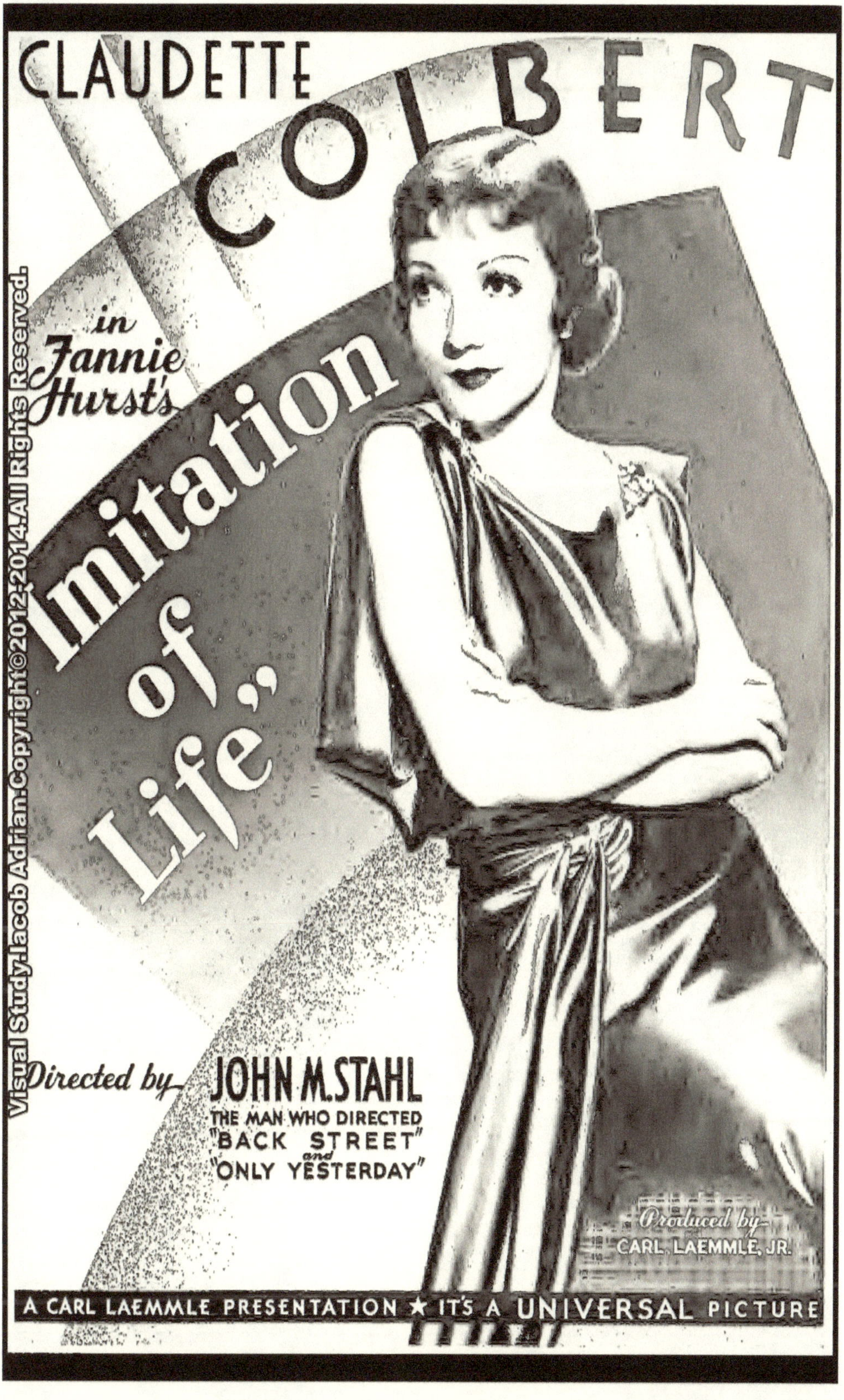

CLAUDETTE COLBERT

in Fannie Hurst's

Imitation of "Life"

Directed by JOHN M. STAHL
THE MAN WHO DIRECTED
"BACK STREET"
and
"ONLY YESTERDAY"

Produced by
CARL LAEMMLE, JR.

A CARL LAEMMLE PRESENTATION ★ IT'S A UNIVERSAL PICTURE

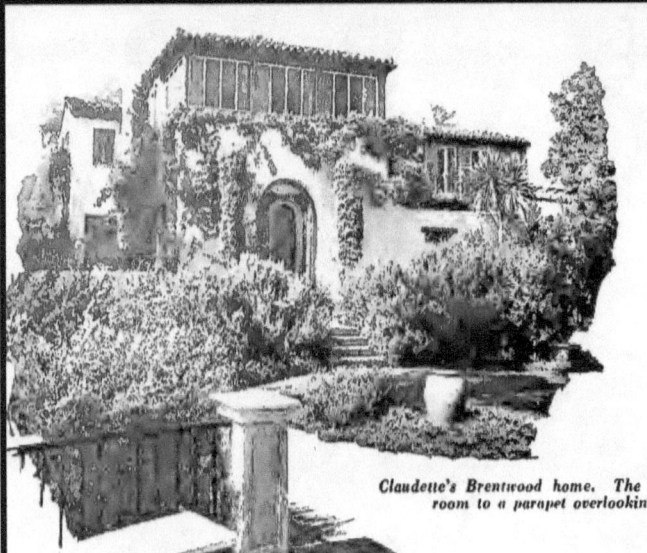

Your first opportunity for an intimate glimpse inside Claudette Colbert's lovely home. Come wander through

with JERRY LANE

Claudette's Brentwood home. The steps lead from the drawing room to a parapet overlooking a flower-filled ravine

LET'S CALL

YOU NEED A MAP, a compass, and a native sense of direction to find Claudette Colbert's house. But when you do find it—oo la la! She took it without bothering to look at the inside. She saw the tiled swimming pool, the tea pergola, the flagstone tennis court, the solid half acre of flowers; she stood on the parapet watching the sunlight on the sea and heard the whispering of the tall eucalyptus trees behind her—and she said, "Sold!" . . . That's Claudette for you. Gloriously impulsive. All a-tingle with life.

But as I drove through the gates and circled up the drive I couldn't help thinking, "I wonder if she knows about the ghost?"

A very nice, lady-like ghost to be sure. A psychic, who had been the chief highlight of a dinner party the evening before, had told me all about her. He had asked us to concentrate on one certain thing and Claudette's house popped into my mind. He turned on me sharply. "It's very beautiful, this place you're thinking of. There is a spirit living there. A gentle little temple dancer who has some connection with an image brought from the far east. . . . She has influenced and helped the young mistress of the house. . . ."

It was a strange story, but I didn't pay much attention to it. Not until I saw the image! There it was, resting on a table in Claudette's drawing room. A scarred antique figure of the Hindu god, Shiva. A companion image, supposedly that of his wife, was at the other end.

Now it's a funny thing about Claudette. She hates mysteries. She'd rather ride an elephant's trunk than read

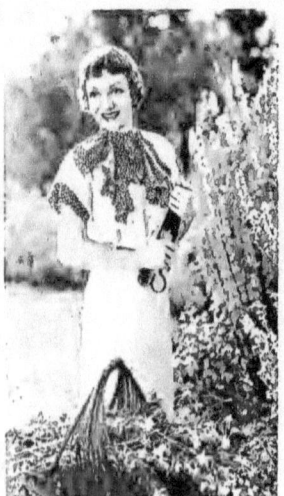

Claudette herself, busy in the flaming gardens which occupy three acres of her estate, which is fifteen miles out of Hollywood

detective stories. And the one time she appeared in a "scare" play—*The Ghost Train*, which choo-chooed on a most successful run along Broadway —she lost twenty pounds. At every performance she frightened herself to death when the green lights flashed on and the head appeared. . . .

What would happen if she knew her house was haunted?

But she doesn't. The playful sprites at Katy Hepburn's hide-away, push the furniture around, and those at Pickfair sometimes keep Mary awake nights. But all Claudette's little temple dancer seems to do is to connive with De Mille to put her in exotic rôles! *Poppaea* in *The Sign of the Cross* and now *Cleopatra*—both of which boosted her stardom stock to the heights.

● "What about those oriental antique figures?" I asked as casually as possible.

"Oh those," she said, and from her tone it was obvious she'd never met her lady ghost guest. It seems she had picked them up in Bali when she and hubby Norman Foster were skylarking around the world. "It was really kind of queer about them," she told me. "I wanted something that was actually old. Everything's so new down there because they build with sandstone and it doesn't last long. I explained to an old crone who looked like a witch what I was searching for. 'I get,' she answered. And she did. The next day she came with something hidden under her apron and here were these images! I'll bet anything she just stole them out of a temple when nobody was looking. . . ."

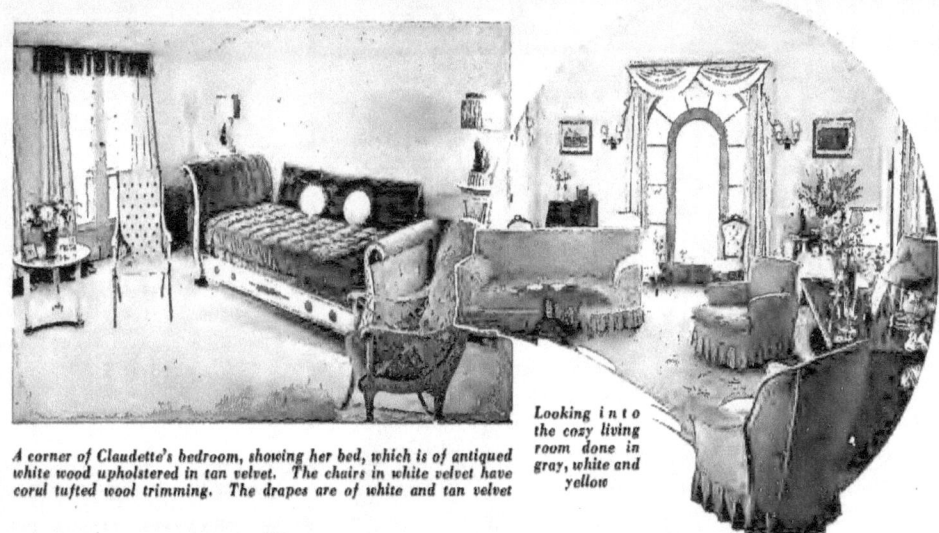

A corner of Claudette's bedroom, showing her bed, which is of antiqued white wood upholstered in tan velvet. The chairs in white velvet have coral tufted wool trimming. The drapes are of white and tan velvet

Looking into the cosy living room done in gray, white and yellow

ON CLAUDETTE

Yes, it *was* queer. Claudette didn't know the half of it!

There's nothing of the mystic or exotic about her. As a matter of fact, she's pretty much the sort of person she played in *It Happened One Night*. Lovable, humorous—all impetuous girl. She married on the spur of the moment. She accepted her first movie offer the same way. And that's the way she moves into houses!

When you see that formal rose bed and enter the spacious tiled hall with its massive pieces you half expect to meet a French duchess. Then you spot the red bicycle nonchalantly parked by the door leading to the patio and you think, "A person of many moods lives here." And of course you're right. Claudette Colbert. . . .

Joan Crawford gave her the bike. But no one sent her the magnificent flowers that are everywhere. They came out of her own garden. And by her orders they're informally arranged, the lowly daisy with the lily, flaming tropical blossoms with demure northern buds. There was a time in New York when she hoarded pennies to buy pots of geraniums to brighten up the small flat she and her mother had. And many a spring day—I'll probably be murdered for this—she used to skip lunch in order to get Mrs. Colbert a bunch of early daffodils. . . .

● Claudette without flowers is a Claudette in a blue funk. There are seven bowls of them in the drawing room alone! In fact, the whole scheme of decoration seems planned as a background for them—the walls are a plain neutral tint, the drapes are white silk rep with a tiny green ball edging, the long Chinese rug is the softest

Another view of Claudette's bedroom, showing the fireplace and large over-mantel mirror. The carpet is white, the walls are cream with tiny brown stripes and the curtains are white organdie, edged with tan balls

of pearl gray tones and has a splash of colored flowers at one end. Against this she has done the unusual; she's covered the great sofa and arm chair on either side of the fireplace with gray corduroy trimmed with white. The two chairs flanking the high window facing the patio have yellow corduroy covers trimmed with gray. Try that in your living room if you want an air of absolute serenity and calm!

Claudette has balanced this with black furniture. And a couple of chairs near the door leading to the terrace are

LET'S MAKE PANCAKES!

You may call them flapjacks, griddlecakes, blinys or crepés but pancakes have what it takes to get by in any language

by

Grace Ellis

HOLLYWOOD'S
Food Consultant

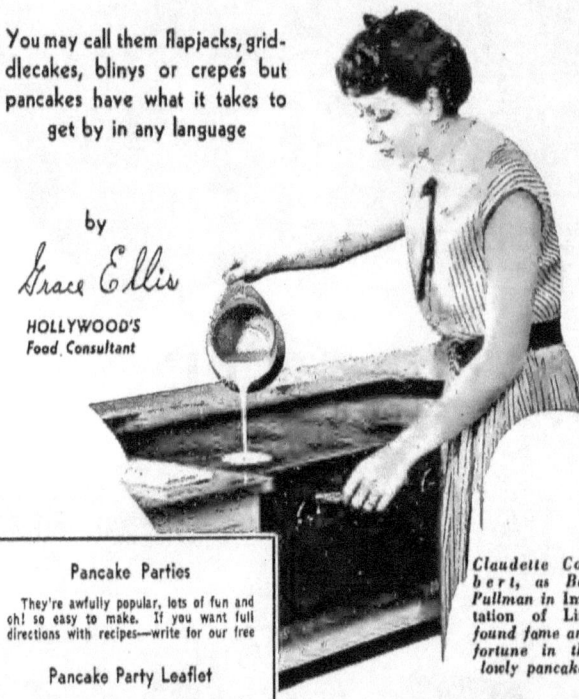

Claudette Colbert, as Bea Pullman in Imitation of Life found fame and fortune in the lowly pancake

HAVE YOU SEEN *Imitation of Life*, starring Claudette Colbert? Rather co-starring Claudette and pancakes! For it's a simple griddlecake recipe which starts Bea Pullman—alias Miss Colbert—on the road to fortune and fame.

But I'll wager that it wasn't that griddlecake recipe which really made the millions. Undoubtedly she *did* have a good recipe but it was the universal masculine urge and love for good home made pancakes, which rang the cash register and made the famous fortune.

They may be "griddlecakes" to you and blinys to a Russian and crêpes to the French but they "have what

it takes" in almost any language. And if you travel round the globe a bit, you'll find that the whole world loves a good pancake.

In America they're a mighty versatile dish. Grandma Gruntly, out at Four Corners, makes them with light flour or dark, with one egg or two, and serves them for breakfast every "spelled-with-an-'r'-month" in the year. Her daughters swear by the new blended pancake flours and the daughter in town finds griddlecakes the perfect answer to that what-shall-I-get-for-supper problem which confronts bridge-playing wives.

And don't be caught curling up your nose at the thought of griddlecakes. Mrs. Ritz on Park Avenue is serving them at formal dinners now-a-days. "Pancakes parties," are popular in Hollywood. And "crêpes," a light pancake rolled round a sprinkling of powdered sugar, plum jelly, or something else just as nonsensical, are considered the smartest sort of adjunct to a morning or afternoon bridge "snack."

So much for the griddlecake social rating.

Now for their making—for family use I like the following recipe:

Million-Dollar Griddlecakes

(A flexible recipe which will turn out a variety of delicious cakes.)

    2   cups flour
    1   teaspoon soda
    ½   teaspoon salt
    1-2 tablespoons sugar
    2   cups sour milk
    1   or 2 well beaten eggs
    2-4 tablespoons melted shortening

Sift the dry ingredients into a deep bowl. Add eggs beaten in with the milk. Add shortening. Blend the mixture with a few deft, quick strokes. Don't try to beat out all the lumps. These will mysteriously disappear during baking. Overmixing causes tough cakes.

Drop mixture by spoonfuls on a greased or ungreased griddle, hot enough to make a few drops of water sputter. Bake until bubbles break on top side. Turn and complete. Serve as soon as possible.

SOUR CREAM MAKES a lighter, more tender cake than sweet. And if you haven't sour milk you can use sweet, and sour it by adding 1 tablespoon of vinegar to each cup of milk. Or use half evaporated milk and half water and use the same amount of vinegar per cup of mixture. If you really prefer a sweet milk griddlecake, then substitute sweet milk for sour and use 3 teaspoons of baking powder in place of the soda called for in the recipe. A very light and fluffy cake is possible if the eggs are separated and the stiffly beaten whites folded in just before the cakes are baked.

Pancakes baked on an ungreased aluminum griddle really need the larger quantity of shortening. And if you like crisp griddlecakes you'll want to use the 4 tablespoons of fat to 2 cups of flour, but if you like soft cakes, baked on a greased griddle, 1 or 2 tablespoons of shortening will be enough. Some women swear by a rich-with-eggs pancake mixture. While some are satisfied with 1 egg to 2 cups of flour. But you can use either 1 or 2 tablespoons of sugar, depending upon whether or not your man-of-the-house likes to get his sweet tooth and his griddlecakes mixed.

THE POINT in making any griddlecake is to have it light and fluffy. Pancakes, like muffins, can be overmixed. I like to sift my dry ingredients into a deep bowl and hollow out a spot for the wet ingredients. Only enough strokes are used in combining the two, to actually dampen the flour. Overbeating, I find, gives a tough rubbery quality which is disappointing to a genuine lover of good cakes.

And don't think that you have to mix your own—if you want real honest to goodness buckwheat cakes. A very new prepared buckwheat pancake flour made possible two memorable occasions recently. At one, a group of husbands, frequently

Let's Make Pancakes!

entertained, retaliated by entertaining their wives—at a pancake party. They did everything themselves, from table-setting to dish-washing. And those buckwheat cakes, made, so they said, from prepared flour, were little less than perfect.

On another occasion old friends dropped in. They were "driving through."—No, they couldn't stop! They *hadn't* had lunch, of course and, to make time they had gone without breakfast. They had to be at so-and-so at such-and-such a time. — You've heard the story as many times as I.

My anguished eyes, roaming my kitchen shelf lighted on the packaged pancake flour. Could they, I begged, stay just thirty minutes. They could! And in fifteen minutes we were seated at a luncheon of chilled pineapple juice —praises be for such things as canned grapefruit and pineapple juice — crisp bacon and "the best buckwheat cakes I've tasted since I was a boy." *That*, from one of the men guests. Credit was due entirely to the flour, since I had merely to add milk and bake.

Another of the group—a woman who manages a highly successful tearoom—was particularly delighted with the pitcher of warm "Honey Cream"—the specialty of another friend—which I had mixed for those not preferring maple syrup. (For Honey Cream, heat 1 cup strained honey until it simmers. Blend well with ½ cup sweet cream, and add a dash of powdered sugar.)

An electric griddle, allowing the pancakes to bake at the table, would have been the crowning touch to such a meal. But in baking cakes on any griddle, I like to test the griddle temperature with a few drops of cold water. As soon as the water sizzles snappily, the griddle is ready for the batter. A thin batter makes light lacy-edged cakes. Thick cakes of the none-too-competent restaurant variety have few devotees.

If a shopping expedition or a session of cards is to keep you from home until shortly before the supper hour, griddlecake batter may be mixed, covered and left in the ice-box ready for instant use on your return. And if you want a two-dish meal which will allow you to toss your hat on a hook at 6:15 and have supper on the table at 6:30, I'd suggest:

Made-In-A-Minute Supper

Ham Griddlecakes   Fresh Fruit Salad
Maple Syrup
Coffee

Prepare the fruit for the salad and make the pancake batter before you leave home.

Ham Griddlecakes. Fry a generous slice of smoked ham to a golden brown on both sides in a greased skillet. Remove bone and fat. Grind in the food chopper. (There should be 1 cup of ground ham.) Add to one recipe of plain griddlecake batter just before cakes are baked.

Crêpes, the French pancakes are essentially a dessert dish. Try them!

Crepes (French Pancakes)

(Makes 6 dessert pancakes)

    2 eggs
    ½ cup milk
    2 tablespoons sugar
    ½ teaspoon salt
    ¼ cup pastry flour

Beat eggs well; add milk. Combine sugar, salt and flour, and add egg mixture gradually stirring just enough to mix. Drop batter by tablespoonfuls on a greased skillet. Cook over a low fire until each cake is a delicate brown on the bottom and firm to the touch on top. Serve with plum jam and thick cream; or sprinkle with powdered sugar and roll. For a bridge dessert, I like to spread the cakes with equal parts of jam and cream mixed. I then roll them, dust with powdered sugar and serve. Try this dessert type of pancake. They're new. And oh, so good!

Other griddlecake variations worth attention are:

Whole Wheat Griddlecakes. Substitute 1 cup whole wheat flour for 1 cup of white flour in the griddlecake recipe. Use 2 tablespoonfuls of molasses mixed into the batter, for sweetening, instead of the sugar.

Cornmeal Griddlecakes. Substitute 1 cup yellow cornmeal for 1 cup of the white flour in the griddlecake recipe. Use brown sugar instead of white. Serve with hot baked ham and maple syrup.

French Pancakes With Sausage. Bake griddlecakes and roll each one around two cooked link sausages, laid end-to-end. Fasten with toothpicks. Arrange on a hot platter. Serve with hot applesauce, and coffee.

Rice Griddlecakes. These are a great favorite in the South. To make them, follow the griddlecake recipe but omit ½ cup of flour and substitute 1 cup of cooked salted rice, mixed with the beaten eggs and milk. Serve with chicken or pork gravy.

Pineapple Griddlecakes. Follow the Million-Dollar Griddlecake recipe but use one cup of drained pineapple juice in place of 1 cup of milk called for, and add 1 cup drained crushed pineapple to the mixed wet ingredients. Sprinkle cakes with powdered sugar when baked. Roll and serve as a dessert.

A ND You Must make Blinys! These are the raised griddlecakes of Russia. But they're considered mighty smart now-a-days for both formal and informal dinners. We've found them excellent as an evening party dish. If you'd like our recipe, and want some suggestions concerning a simple, inexpensive and just awfully popular method of entertaining friends write for the free leaflet, "Pancake Parties." Address Grace Ellis, Foods Editor, HOLLYWOOD Magazine, 529 South 7th St., Minneapolis, Minnesota, enclosing a stamped addressed envelope.

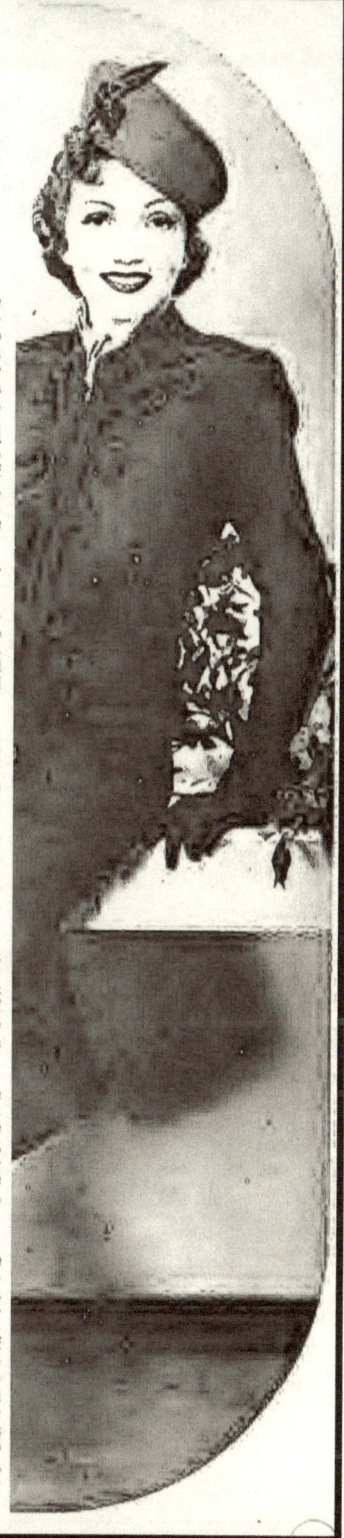

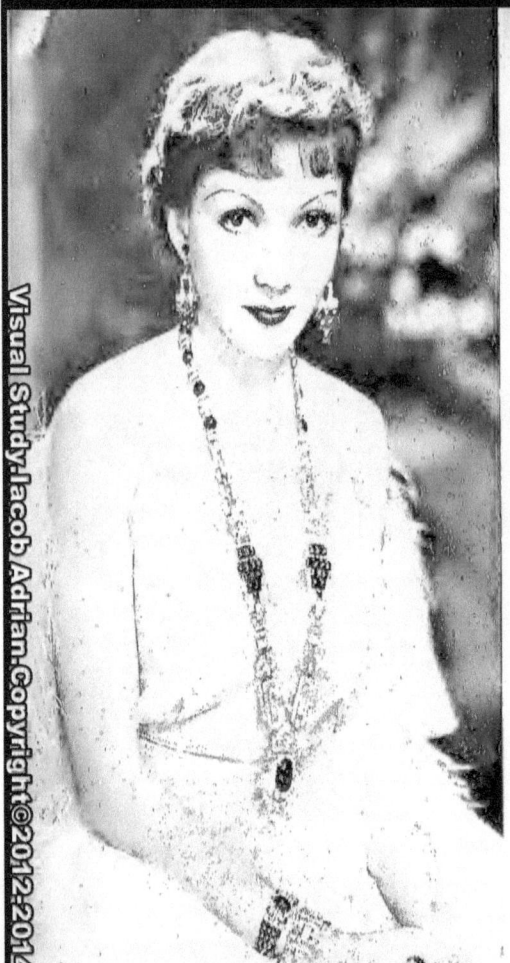

The *Secret*

by *Claudette Colbert*

How Nice It would be if a woman could but glance at a man and know just how to classify him!

Of course, every woman *tries* to do that. She tucks him neatly into what she think is his proper pigeon-hole, all carefully labeled, gives him a little pat and says: "There you are, that's where *you* belong!"

But when you think you have put your finger on one of the species, and triumphantly decide that he is an introvert with a love for peace and comfort, he's apt to break out in an affair of fisticuffs at a night-club—and then where are you?

Perhaps that's what I like about men. The unexpected is always interesting.

To approach the study of this fascinating subject of fascinating them, I believe I should begin with the observation that men are not so dumb as they are painted. Oh no, really, they are a clever lot! Yet most women make the mistake of assuming that all males are both thick-skinned and obtuse.

Women will come out with the most bare-faced flattery—something you would hesitate to hand a six-year-old child—and expect instant results.

It is embarrassing to a man to be made the object of blatant flattery. The unfortunate fellow, being cursed with notions of chivalry that prevent him from bursting out with a terse retort, must pretend, instead, to swallow it all. He must stand there like a fool and draw circles with his toe and say, "Aw, you don't mean it," and be fully aware that you *don't*. Flattery is very apt to back-fire, when used injudiciously upon men. If you would succeed with men, give them credit for intelligence.

● If I were to pick out Rule Number One for a girl who has set her saucy cap for some particular man, I would say: *The first thing to do is to find out what his particular interests are.*

Once you know his likes and dislikes, it is not difficult to make yourself agreeable in his eyes. Should you blindly assume that he is, being a man, interested in football, you might prattle on about teams and standings and All-American quarterbacks for hours before discovering that he is utterly bored with football.

In my recent picture, *Imitation of Life*, a revealing incident developed to point a moral in this respect. Warren William played the part of my suitor, a wealthy ichthyologist. Eager to make a commendable impression upon him, Rochelle Hudson, as my daughter, scurried off to look up the word "ichthyologist" in the dictionary, and then attempted to discuss the subject of fishes with him.

Quite the proper technique! Unfortunately, the study of fish is not so simple as it sounds, and should you ever confront an ichthyologist, don't try to dazzle him with hurriedly crammed knowledge of his pet subject!

But it is true that the first step in charming a man is to find out what he likes.

This is a subtle form of flattery that can excite no objections. If you do a man the honor of

ARE YOU ATTRACTIVE TO MEN?

Check up on your good points with this chart prepared in collaboration with Miss Colbert. A perfect score is 100—but, remember, no man desires perfection! In estimating your own values, set down the figures in the outside column. Or ask your most critical friend to make out your score.

PHYSICAL BEAUTY

	Value	Your Score
Does your coiffure emphasize your good points?	10	
Is your complexion good, your make-up blended?	10	
Are your teeth straight and kept white?	10	
Have you kept your weight close to normal?	10	
Hands, nails—are they perfectly groomed?	3	
Do your clothes heighten your appeal?	7	

MENTAL ATTRIBUTES

	Value	Your Score
Is your disposition cheerful, variable, or gloomy?	10	
In your presence are men at ease, awkward, or glum?	10	
Can you discuss masculine topics, or only recipes?	5	
Do men like to talk to you?	5	
Do you rely on sex appeal or include mental appeal?	5	
Have you read two new books and today's sport section?	5	
Can you flatter a man without his realising it?	10	

Ideal total ....100 points. Your score:......

# of CHARMING MEN

You need more than beauty to attract some men, more than personality to attract others. But Claudette tells how any girl can make herself attractive to any man, no matter who he is. Can you pass her test of a woman's appeal?

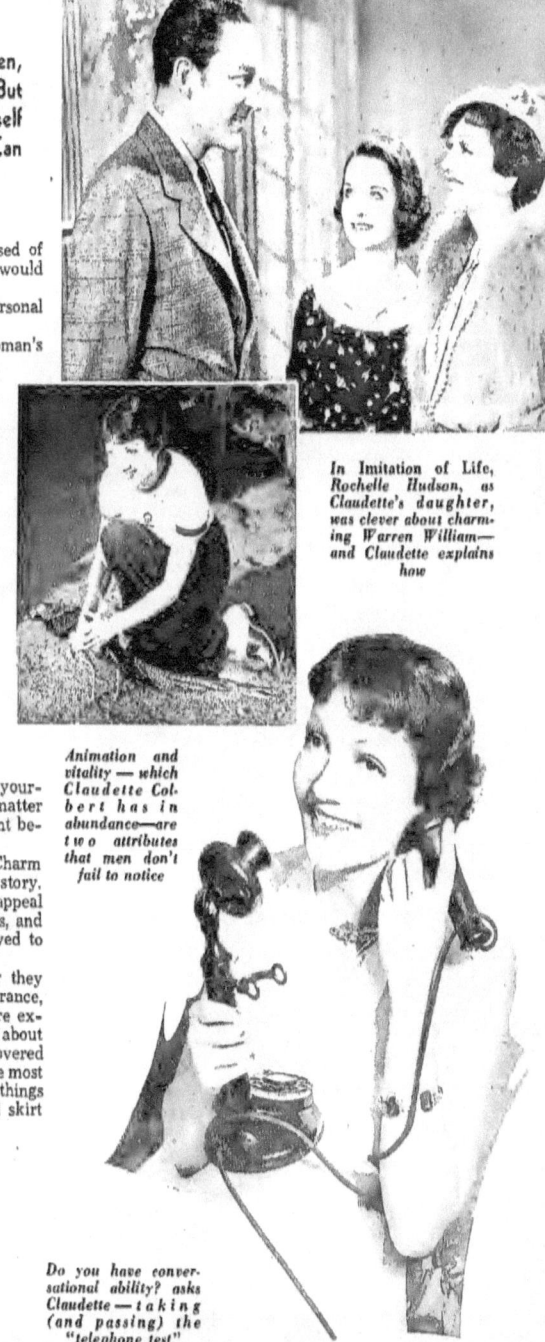

In Imitation of Life, Rochelle Hudson, as Claudette's daughter, was clever about charming Warren William—and Claudette explains how

Animation and vitality — which Claudette Colbert has in abundance—are two attributes that men don't fail to notice

Do you have conversational ability? asks Claudette — taking (and passing) the "telephone test"

discussing his hobbies, you may rightfully be accused of deliberately trying to please him, but certainly he would be the last to object to this form of cozening.

From that point on, success depends upon your personal attraction.

I believe that no normal man can overlook a woman's neglect to make herself physically attractive. With all due respect for mental qualifications, a woman must remember that men see, as well as hear, and that all the pearls of wisdom that fall from the lips of a physically unattractive woman will fail to blind his eyes.

Fortunately, you do not have to be beautiful to charm a man. Even women who would be judged homely by classical standards are often very attractive to men.

The whole thing condenses to this: Make the most of what you have.

● It has always amused me that I should be considered beautiful, for I have looked at myself too often in the mirror. At the same time, I am secretly pleased to discover how I have managed to fool people on that score. You see, I place such credit where it belongs—on my determination to make the best of my good points.

That, surely, is practical advice, is it not?

For, consider—you can apply your rouge in the morning, deftly, carefully, and in a moment fool even yourself into thinking how well you look, when as a matter of fact you may have felt positively haggard a moment before.

And now I discover that I am leading up to the Charm Chart that the editor suggests should appear with my story. In arriving at this chart with him, I said that physical appeal should rate just as high as other feminine attractions, and by the same token, other attributes cannot be allowed to add up to more than physical allure.

But in this category I would include clothes, for they are most certainly an indispensable part of your appearance, at least in present-day society. The *right* clothes are exceedingly important. I have experienced one reaction about clothes from men that has surprised me. I have discovered that when I wore severely tailored suits, men would be most impressed with my appearance. Not feminine, frilly things at all, as one might expect, but a little jacket and skirt seemed to make the biggest hit. They would come up and say: "How smart you look in that!"

Now, you would think that tailored clothes would detract from your femininity. Take my word for it, some women look more feminine in smartly tailored outfits than they do in laces and flounces.

If you doubt that observation on the reactions of the observant male,

This Happened One Night with Mlle. CLAUDETTE

Monsieur Boyer remembers Lily Chauchoin's mud pack

by

Charles Boyer

● THEY GAVE HER a slender, gold statuette for being the most outstanding actress of the year, this little Claudette Colbert. It is the highest award Hollywood has to offer.

But there's another award I'd like to give her. So, I think, would everyone who knows her, who has ever worked with her. An award for being the most natural, regular person in the whole of Hollywood!

How she has managed it, I don't know. Perhaps that is why, to me, she is such a surprising girl. Such an amazing, brilliant woman.

Here she is—one of the most famous women on earth, a great star. Yet the hubbub of the town has never touched her. Neither its quick gossip nor its headlines. It takes strength to build up for yourself a world of peace and normalcy in abnormal surroundings. It takes courage to live in it! Claudette has done both.

I met her for the first time three years ago when I played with her and Clive Brook in *The Man from Yesterday.* She came on the set, a slim young girl who looked typically French, who spoke it with the purest of accents—the accent of Tours—and who *thought* in American! To a Frenchman like myself, it was bewildering. . . . Finding a girl who could meet a man on his own ground and was still so feminine. . . . Who had that subtle charm of the Parisian and the sportsmanship of the Yankee. It's a wonderful combination. And when you add to it richly developed humor—that's Claudette!

● IN THOSE DAYS, I was a stranger, struggling with a new language. She and her mother, Mrs. Chauchoin, proved a god-send in helping me to learn English. Occasionally they invited me for dinner in the home they had taken at the Outpost estates. It was there I was introduced to Claudette's real little world. The world that includes besides her mother, her aunt, her brother Charles and his wife and as many friends as she can crowd in and still do justice to them all. For friendship is something sacred to Claudette. The kind that is remarkably loyal and enduring.

Sometimes you hear her called, even by those who know her best, a "dual personality." That is not true. It's simply that like all other fascinating women she is many-sided.

I remember an incident that happened shortly before I left for France.

I had dined with the Colberts and all evening she had been speaking about the picture Cecil deMille was to make, *The Sign of the Cross.* She was eager to do Poppaea, wicked Roman empress. And as she spoke, you could feel the fire and drama in her voice, the hidden flame that is in the girl. She was Claudette, the enchantress, then.

Later, all of us went to the second show at a nearby theatre. There was the usual comedy and in this one the heroine's face was liberally splashed with mud.

"There!" chortled Claudette. "That's the way I look best—with a mud pack!" And this laughing, teasing small girl was the same person who had been the enchantress such a short while before! Oh but she is versatile, this one! And the little-girl Claudette has her own appeal, too.

I returned to Paris and it was three years before I saw her again. Much can happen in that time. It did to her.

Claudette flashed into infinitely greater brilliance. She had success such as few people dare to dream of. I had left her doing a succession of "nice girl" rôles. Suddenly she switched into parts as many-sided as herself. France went mad over her Poppaea, over the winsome comédienne of *It Happened One Night*—called *New York-Miami* over there.

Would such sensational fame change her? Could it *help* but change her? I wondered.

● SOMETIMES I SENT new French books to her mother since they're hard to get in the United States. I had been married in the meanwhile and when my wife, Pat Paterson, cabled me our new Hollywood address I found she had taken Claudette's old home in the Outpost Estates! Outside of that I had no contact with the Colberts. Not until that day, quite recently, when I walked onto the stage to do *Private Worlds* with the Claudette the whole world was talking about.

At least that gay smile of hers was the same! So was her simple, friendly manner with the entire crew, with the extras. And as we went on working together day after day other little personality-revealing t h i n g s cropped up. For instance, Claudette learned that the script girl had been ill and that she needed specially prepared food. The next day at noontime I saw her quietly [Continued on page 59]

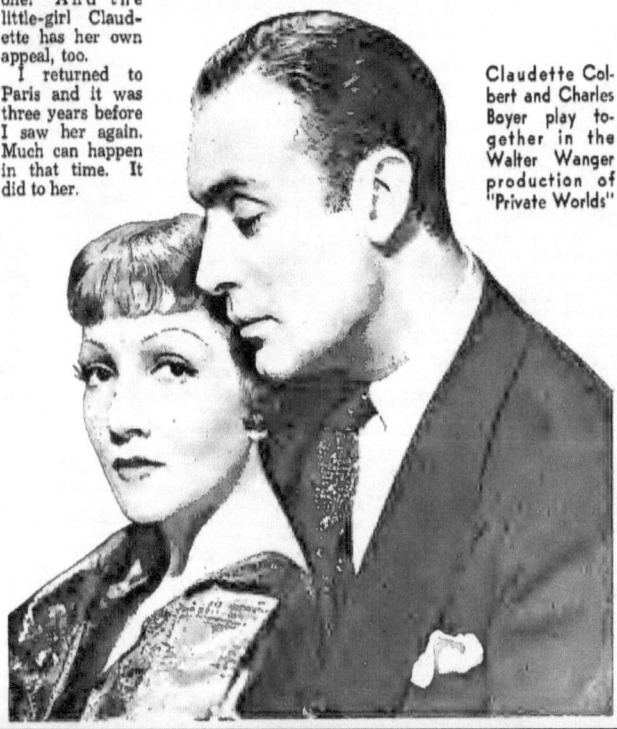

Claudette Colbert and Charles Boyer play together in the Walter Wanger production of "Private Worlds"

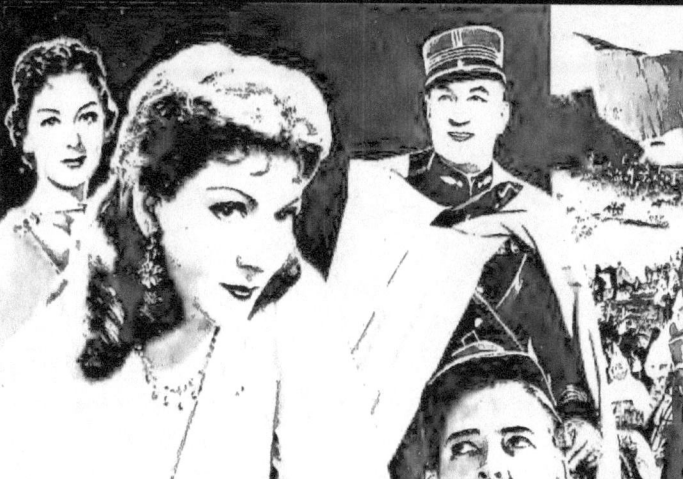

Love

as burning as Sahara's Sands

From Ouida's romantic novel of the French Foreign Legion, flashes this glorious spectacle-drama of men's heroism and women's devotion, enacted by one of the greatest casts the screen has ever seen.

UNDER TWO FLAGS

starring

Ronald

COLMAN
(Beau Geste)

featuring

Claudette

COLBERT
(It Happened One Night)

VICTOR
McLAGLEN
(The Informer)

ROSALIND
RUSSELL
(Rendezvous)

with GREGORY RATOFF • NIGEL BRUCE • C. HENRY GORDON • HERBERT MUNDIN

AND A CAST OF 10,000

a DARRYL F. ZANUCK 20th CENTURY PRODUCTION
(Les Miserables .. House of Rothschild)

Presented by Joseph M. Schenck
Directed by Frank Lloyd *(Cavalcade .. Mutiny on the Bounty)*
Associate Producer Raymond Griffith • Based on the novel by Ouida

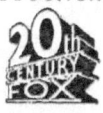

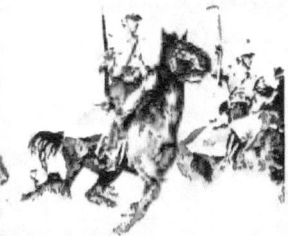

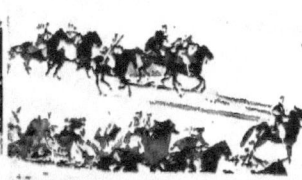

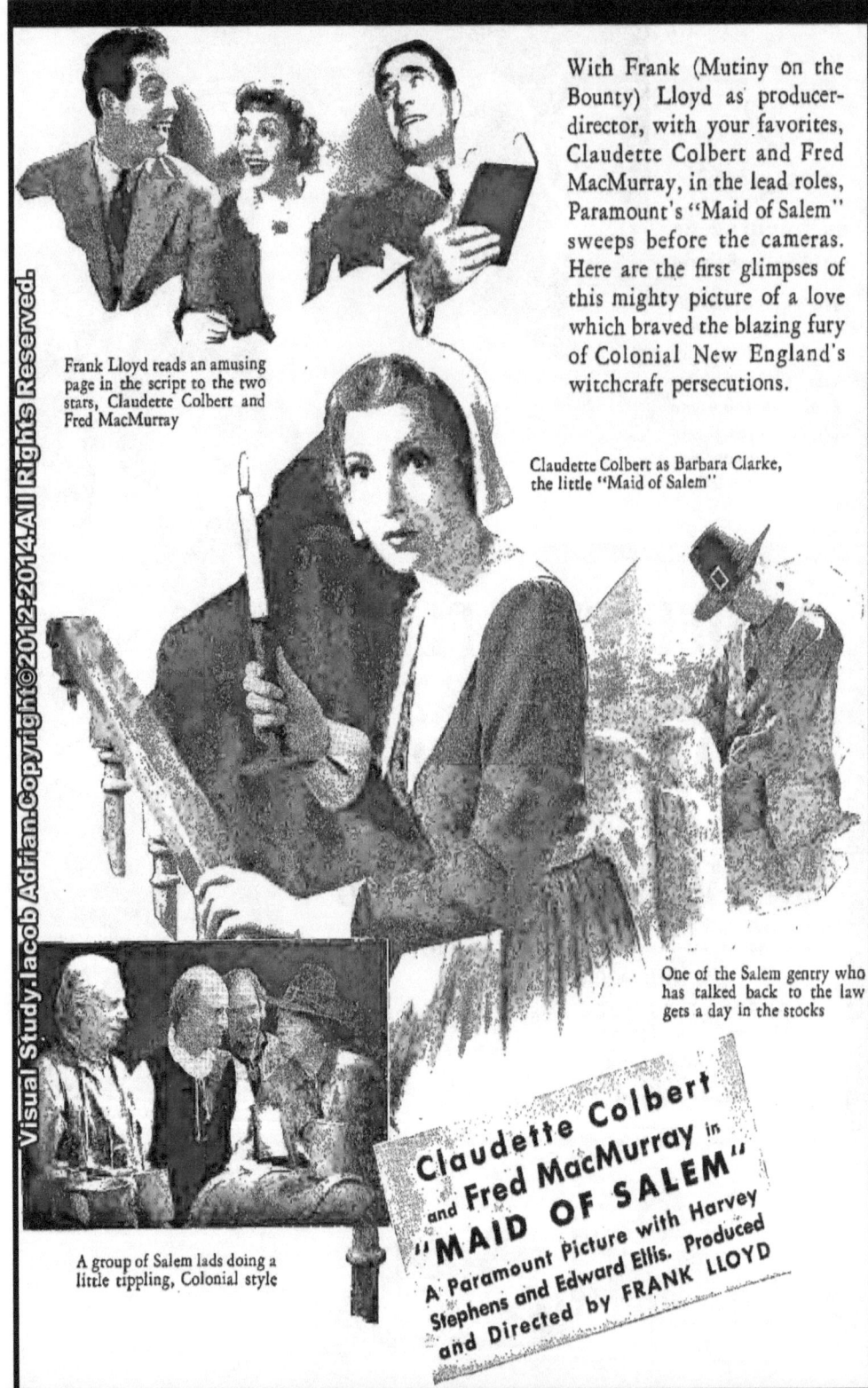

With Frank (Mutiny on the Bounty) Lloyd as producer-director, with your favorites, Claudette Colbert and Fred MacMurray, in the lead roles, Paramount's "Maid of Salem" sweeps before the cameras. Here are the first glimpses of this mighty picture of a love which braved the blazing fury of Colonial New England's witchcraft persecutions.

Frank Lloyd reads an amusing page in the script to the two stars, Claudette Colbert and Fred MacMurray

Claudette Colbert as Barbara Clarke, the little "Maid of Salem"

One of the Salem gentry who has talked back to the law gets a day in the stocks

A group of Salem lads doing a little tippling, Colonial style

Claudette Colbert and Fred MacMurray in "MAID OF SALEM" A Paramount Picture with Harvey Stephens and Edward Ellis. Produced and Directed by FRANK LLOYD

They'd Hang Claudette for a Witch!

CLAUDETTE COLBERT is by nature a gay and sparkling young lady. That was one of the main reasons why they were getting ready to hang her on the gallows a fortnight ago—hang her by the neck until dead. The gallows were built. The death sentence had been passed. And Claudette was actually standing there gazing in horror at the rope!

It looked very bad. Our arrival apparently did no good. The hangman was going about his task. (No, this isn't a dream!) The crowds gathered around, and they weren't movie fans looking for autographs. This was a wild mob!

And just when things looked blackest, our hero came to the rescue. Pushing his way through the shouting mob was Fred MacMurray (cavalier this time, and not a Texas Ranger). In short order Fred ended the whole thing and saved the life of beautiful, vivacious Claudette.

It seemed like a narrow escape, but Director Frank Lloyd, looking at his synopsis once in a while to be sure what picture he was s h o o t i n g, knew all the time that so lovely a maiden could never be hanged on the charge of being a witch!

Maid of Salem is perhaps the most unusual picture of the season for Paramount. It deals with witchcraft and popular superstition in the year of 1692, but for all its weird theme, *Maid of Salem* is not morbid.

Although for awhile it looked like *Maid of Salem* was going to be terribly delayed due to Claudette's untimely head bump, things are working out now. Jolted when her car was bumped by a taxi, the star sustained a brain concussion that sent her doctor-husband rushing back from New York by airplane. The concussion was severe but not dangerous, once recognized and treated.

Claudette Colbert's personality is largely responsible for this saving grace. True, she is a Puritan maid in a straight-laced New England colony. But her Pilgrim's costume makes her cuter than ever, and she fairly sparkles all over the place. She

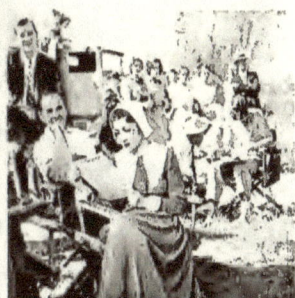

Claudette misses her bangs in this picture, but of course she can't have them. They weren't worn in the pioneer days!

loves informality. That makes the period between shots something liveable for all.

Trust the Doctor!

For instance, there before us was the scene between Harvey Stephens, the village doctor, and herself. He was finishing a quotation from a 1690 medical book ...

"Purge the patient daily, and make him comfortable. And with the grace of God he may recover."

Claudette looks up demurely.

"If you get help from Him, why bother to pay the doctor?" she asks the physician.

"Most people don't," Dr. Stephens assures her.

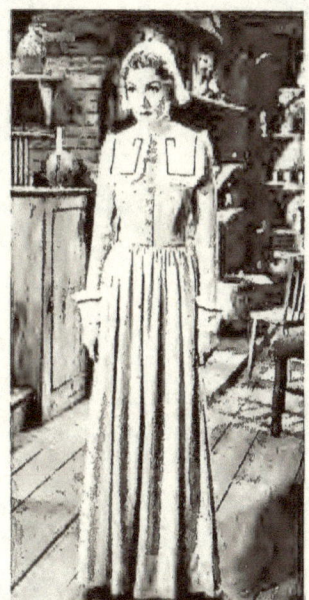

Meet the *Maid of Salem!* In this picture Claudette gets into trouble because her laughing eyes don't fit Puritan ideals

Then he hands her a new bonnet he brought her from Boston. (All the time silence reigns, cameras grind, lights glitter. And Director Lloyd watches intently.)

Claudette takes the bonnet over to a 1692 version of what is now laughingly called a mirror. She tries to put the hat on, gazing into the asserted mirror. Suddenly she straightens up and faces Director Lloyd. "Am I supposed to be able to see myself in this gol-wholloping hunk of glass?" she demands.

"Cut!" says Director Lloyd with a nod to the cameraman. "Who got so darned

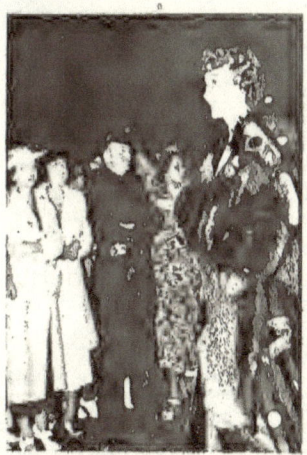

Claudette Colbert smiles for the crowd—and why not? She's by nature a happy, gay creature

literal as that? Of course she has to see herself!"

Lloyd, Miss Colbert and Stephens adjourn to a corner while property men run for a practical mirror.

Another Big Picture

Over in the corner they are talking about a picture which Lloyd will direct for Claudette in the spring. It's the film version of *I, James Lewis*.

Claudette wanted to do that story as long as a year ago. She couldn't muster up much interest around Paramount, however. About that time she was called over to 20th Century-Fox to play the rôle of Cigarette in *Under Two Flags*. Frank Lloyd was the director. During an odd moment she told him of her intense desire to be in the screen version of the story.

Lloyd, too, had read *I, James Lewis*. And had the same reaction. More than anything else, he wanted to direct the film version, along the sweeping lines of his now famous *Mutiny on the Bounty*.

"Our thoughts along those lines were interrupted by Cigarette's untimely death in *Under Two Flags*," Lloyd said. "And by the way, the manner in which she handled her demise is something I'm still raving about. I don't like death scenes—hate to direct them. This thing loomed at me most menacingly. When we dragged up the cameras and Claudette collapsed in Ronald Colman's arms, I couldn't think of a suggestion to give them.

"And they didn't need any. Claudette died like a veteran. Honestly, my mouth dropped open. It was better than I ever hoped for. Did you bawl, too, when she passed away on the desert?"

Claudette interrupted him modestly with this crack: "That scene was the easiest of all. On location in the desert is a real trial. With all that heat, all I had to do was give way to my feelings. I felt like dying. All you had to do was grind off the film."

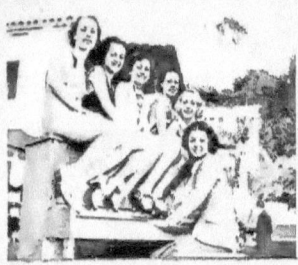

They dance, they swim—and they sing! These pretty chorines were guests of Frances Langford, seated at the piano. From the left: Dot Sanders, Vivian Faulkner, Jaqueline Dax, Midgie Dare, Jean Ashton

They'd Hang Claudette for a Witch!

But back to the James Lewis picture. Lloyd was adopted by Paramount recently and given *Maid of Salem* as his first assignment. Directing Claudette brings joy to any director's heart. But he was even more over-joyed to find he would direct her next film, and it would be *I, James Lewis*. They're still congratulating themselves.

Maid of Salem works a few hardships on Claudette, to her way of thinking. For one thing, she has been temporarily deprived of her bangs. And although it does not change her beauty in the slightest, she feels a little unkindly toward the unidentified person who pointed out bangs weren't just the thing in 1692.

And then again, her fingers can't be manicured in modern fashion. They have to be Puritan-ish, with close-clipped, uncolored nails. And she simply must not say "can't" for "cannot" in the script. Her English has to revert 250 years.

For a Puritan girl, Claudette clowns most amazingly. In one scene she was supposed to do a dance with an imaginary partner—one of the reasons why they decided she was a witch. Now, Claudette dances divinely when actually in the arms of a handsome gentlemen, but it is a little strain on her credulity to react in exactly the same way without a partner.

So she started clowning. As an off stage proposition this appealed to Director Lloyd. He left his easy chair and made a valiant attempt to out-clown Claudette. The audience of grips and juicers applauded while time was a-waiting. After the fun Claudette settled down and did the scene better than any boss could ask for.

Since we have aroused your curiosity somewhat about the new picture, *Maid of Salem*, we will reveal this much. Claudette, the Puritan, is a rebel at heart. She meets Fred MacMurray, a Virginian with a price on his head for inciting revolt down south. His chivalry and gaiety is a strange contrast to New England prudery. So of course she falls in love with him during their clandestine meetings in the forest.

Finally, in the midst of a witch scare which has already seen the execution of nineteen persons, Claudette is singled out because of her strange actions (a nice Puritan never acted like she was really in love, you know.) And through the schemings of an irresponsible child (Bonita Granville), Claudette is brought to trial.

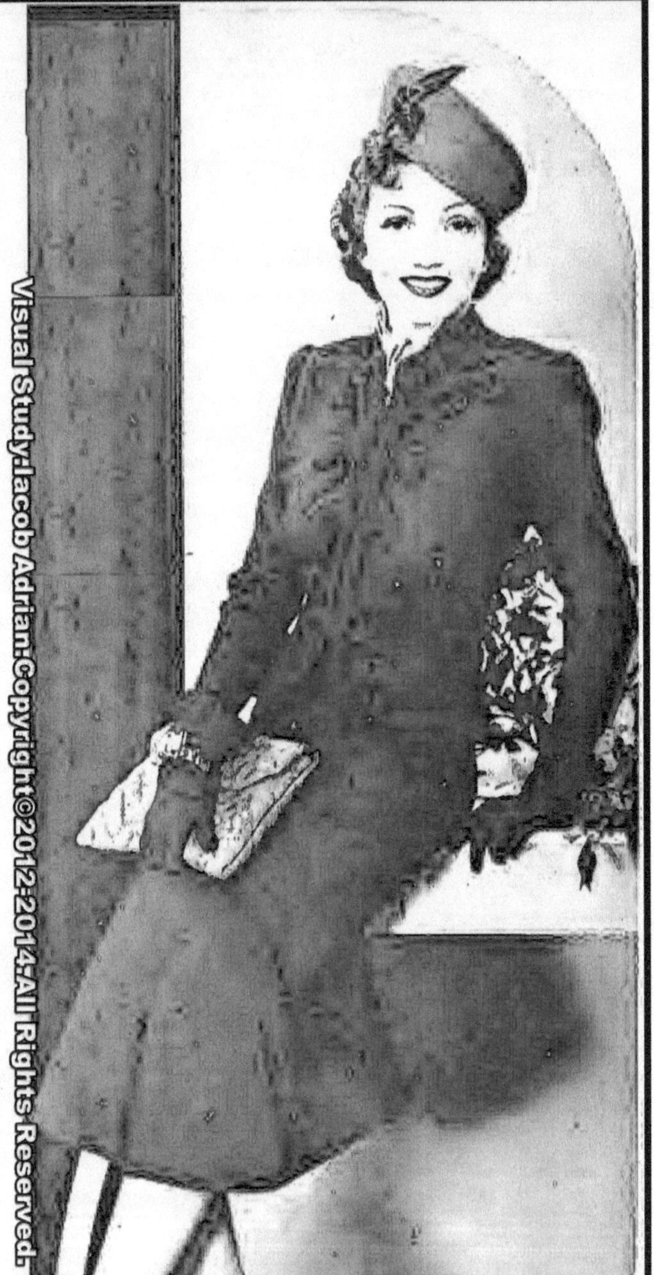

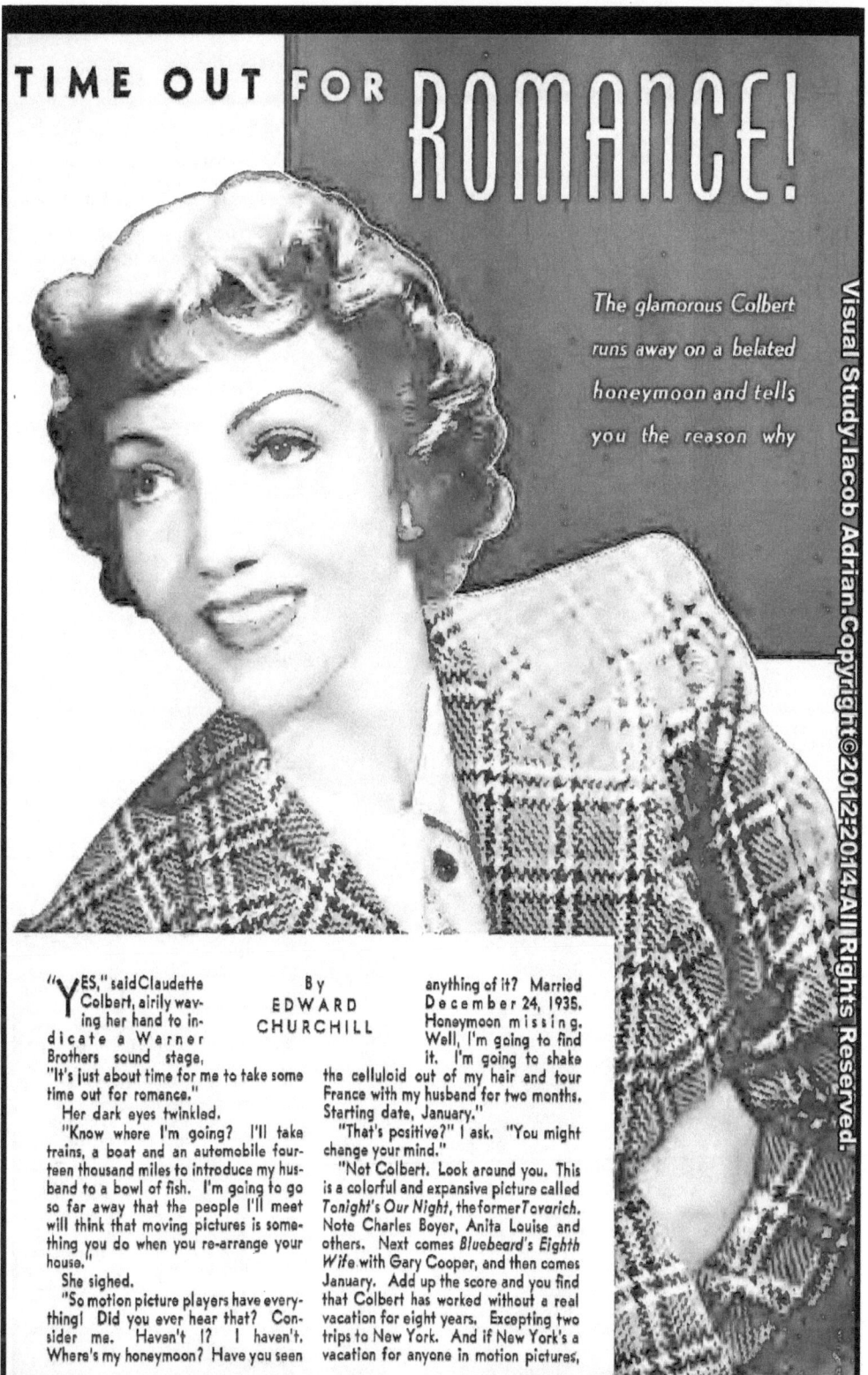

TIME OUT FOR ROMANCE!

The glamorous Colbert runs away on a belated honeymoon and tells you the reason why

"YES," said Claudette Colbert, airily waving her hand to indicate a Warner Brothers sound stage, "It's just about time for me to take some time out for romance."

Her dark eyes twinkled.

"Know where I'm going? I'll take trains, a boat and an automobile fourteen thousand miles to introduce my husband to a bowl of fish. I'm going to go so far away that the people I'll meet will think that moving pictures is something you do when you re-arrange your house."

She sighed.

"So motion picture players have everything! Did you ever hear that? Consider me. Haven't I? I haven't. Where's my honeymoon? Have you seen

By
EDWARD
CHURCHILL

anything of it? Married December 24, 1935. Honeymoon missing. Well, I'm going to find it. I'm going to shake the celluloid out of my hair and tour France with my husband for two months. Starting date, January."

"That's positive?" I ask. "You might change your mind."

"Not Colbert. Look around you. This is a colorful and expansive picture called *Tonight's Our Night*, the former *Tovarich*. Note Charles Boyer, Anita Louise and others. Next comes *Bluebeard's Eighth Wife* with Gary Cooper, and then comes January. Add up the score and you find that Colbert has worked without a real vacation for eight years. Excepting two trips to New York. And if New York's a vacation for anyone in motion pictures,

I'm Shirley Temple. New York's just East Hollywood. We'll have to go through it. New York's a lovely place, too. I can imagine nothing better than seeing it after being shipwrecked on a two-by-four island. But when you enter from the Hollywood side, that's something else again. And Hollywood's nice, too," she continued. "I like going out. It has some nice surroundings. Consider Pebble Beach, Del Monte, Carmel. But they're just around the corner, after all.

"Or the cafes and night clubs. I can see where out-of-town visitors love them. But after eight years, it's like taking a vacation in a studio commissary."

HER attitude isn't hard to understand, after all. Work's work, and even if you're behind a soda fountain, you find the ice cream gets tiresome.

"Consider the highways and byways of France," she went on. "Consider me on a pair of skis floundering down the Austrian Alps. Maybe yodeling a bit, even. Visiting Paris and Le Blanc, both places filled with childhood memories. Recapturing and reliving things the years have taken away."

Claudette confesses that though she was born in Paris and spent five summers in the quaint little town of Le Blanc, on the banks of the river La Creuse, she doesn't know the French countryside—and wants to get acquainted with it.

Entering into this delightful scheme for escape, of course, is Claudette's husband, Dr. Joel D. Pressman.

"It's not my trip, but our trip," she explains. "Jack, born in Philadelphia and educated in the east, has never been abroad. Not only that, but he hasn't had a vacation in fifteen years.

"We've got our honeymoon coming to us. We slipped away, remember, one December day—Christmas Eve, some two years ago—and drove to Yuma. It was an elopement, and we dodged reporters, hurried home so I could go to work in *Under Two Flags* and Jack could fulfill his professional obligations.

"It seemed ironic when, after rushing back to work, I found myself ordered to return to the Yuma desert and live there for two weeks while making *Under Two Flags*. Jack couldn't get away to come down to see me."

BUT back to the proposed honeymoon. I asked about the fish she mentions.

"Bouillabaise," she replies. "The trip'll end in Marseilles. Jack'll eat bouillabaise there. I've been telling him about it for years. He'll get to sample it at last."

"How do you spell it? Can't I just call it fish?"

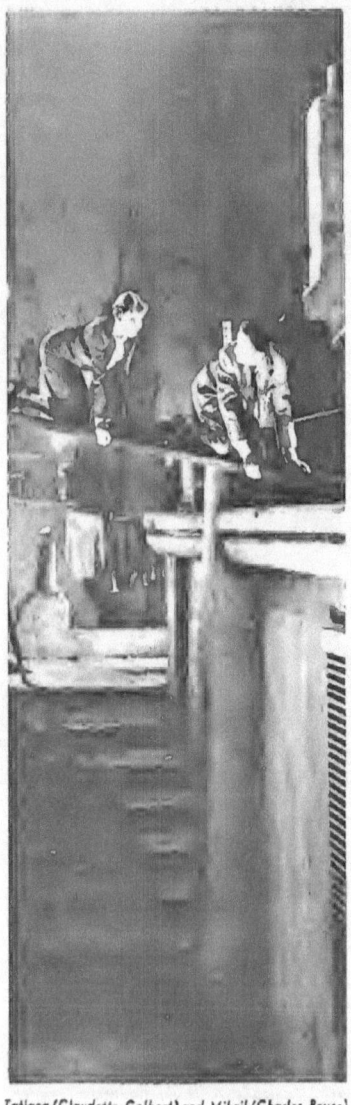

Tatiana (Claudette Colbert) and Mikail (Charles Boyer) in a scene in Warner Bros. screen version of Tovarich

She writes it down for me.

"You can get fish anywhere. You get bouillabaise only in Marseilles."

She had a faraway look in her eyes. I think France has her again. But no.

"Funny the way, when you love someone," she confides, "you think of places you've been alone, and talk about them, and want that person to see them. I've been talking Paris and France to Jack for months. There are so many things I not only want to see for myself, but show him." She smiles.

"Jack has to see La Blanc," she says. "I haven't been there since I was five. Or six. We used to leave the apartment in Paris in the summer time and go to grandfather Chauchoin's place in 'la villa haute,' or the high part of town. The river cut the village in half, and 'le ville bas' was on the other side of beautiful La Creuse, the river."

She laughs suddenly.

CLAUDETTE has places in Paris to show her husband. Quaint little places which have gathered mellowness with the passing of the years.

"We lived in an apartment near the Bois de Bologne," she recalls. "It was like Central Park—a little bit—and I used to play there. In later trips I saw other places, other things, all beautiful. There's another thing I want to do, and that's call on a friend of my father's named Pascaud.

"Not long ago he sent my mother and me a picture of my father, who died in 1924, as a young man. We treasure it, and I want to thank him. And I want to talk to him about my father, too. There'll be other old friends to see, other pleasant hours to be brought back to life."

Claudette feels a common emotion—an affection for the place of her birth.

"I'm a little afraid, though—" she says. "Maybe I've told Jack too much about it, and maybe, when he sees it, he won't have the feeling I do because there won't be any strong associations attached to it. I hope I haven't over-talked it all."

Claudette and her husband are really going to tour France. They're shipping over their small coupe, and they're going to stay off the main highways.

"He'll probably gain about twenty pounds," she says. "He loves to eat—and when he gets some real French food—"

She pauses and eyes me rather skeptically.

"Do you realize what a thrill I'm getting just thinking about all this—and how I really feel?" she asks.

"Of course I do," I reply.

THE MOST EXCITING SCREEN EVENT OF ALL TIME!

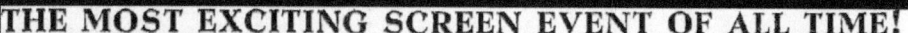

The favorite play of America is
THE SCREEN-HIT OF THE YEAR!

A year of preparation—3 months before the cameras—production costs breaking all studio records—and now the-love-and-laughter show that enthralled New York and London stage audiences for two seasons is ready to flash its glories on the nation's screens.

"Tonight's our night —there may never ..."

WARNER BROS. present:

Claudette **COLBERT**

Charles **BOYER**

in the most lovable, laughable comedy of a decade!

"TOVARICH"

supported by a huge cast of famous stars including

BASIL RATHBONE
☆ ANITA LOUISE ☆

MELVILLE COOPER • ISABEL JEANS
MORRIS CARNOVSKY • VICTOR KILIAN • Directed by
Anatole Litvak • Screen play by Casey Robinson • Adapted
from the play by Jacques Deval • English Version by Robert E.
Sherwood • Music by Max Steiner • A Warner Bros. Picture

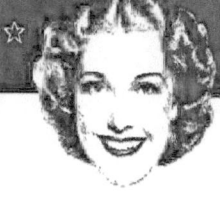
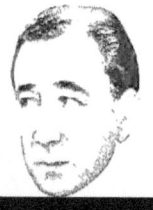
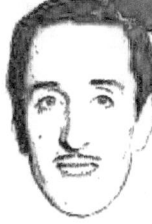

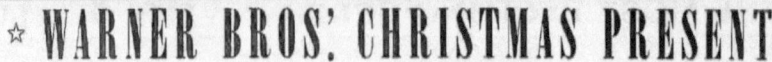

☆ WARNER BROS' CHRISTMAS PRESENT

A million dollars worth of fun

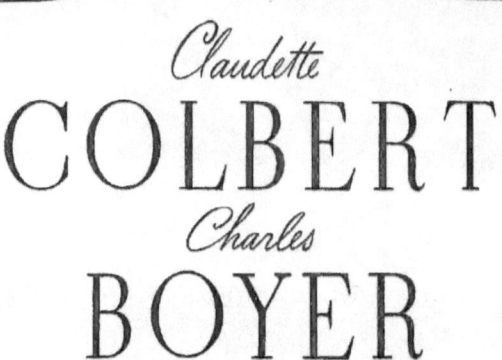

Claudette
COLBERT

Charles
BOYER

in

THE SEASON'S MOST EXCITING SCREEN EVENT

TOVARICH

The show that gave Paris a new sensation, thrilled London, and captured New York ... now in the full glory of the screen's mighty magic ... with a great cast of supporting stars including

BASIL RATHBONE
ANITA LOUISE

MELVILLE COOPER • ISABEL JEANS

MORRIS CARNOVSKY • VICTOR KILIAN • An ANATOLE LITVAK Production
Screen play by Casey Robinson • Adapted from the play by Jacques Deval • English
Version by Robert E. Sherwood • Music by Max Steiner • A Warner Bros. Picture

☆

It's on the way to your favorite theatre now — the grandest
love and laughter picture of this or any other year! ... A
glorious Christmas treat for a hundred million movie-goers.

D THE WHOLE WIDE WORLD! ☆

lamour and romance!

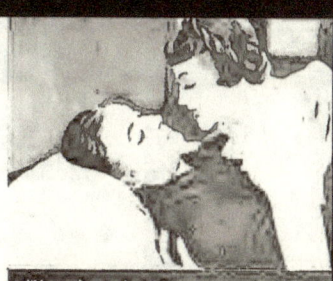

"Yesterday is done! Tomorrow—who knows?
... Tonight's our night!"

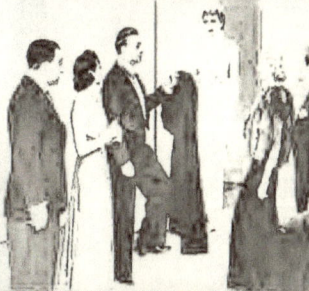

Ready for a gala night in Paris! ... with 4 billion
francs in the bank—and not a sou they could call
their own!

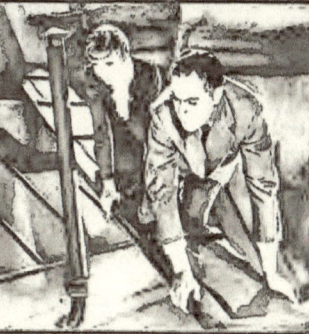

The runaway lovers take to the roof in one of
the amusing and amazing scenes in "Tovarich."

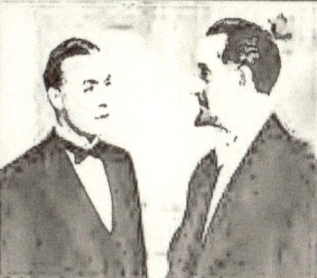

"TOVARICH" is full of big moments—and
here's one as Charles Boyer comes face to face
with that suave villain ... Basil Rathbone.

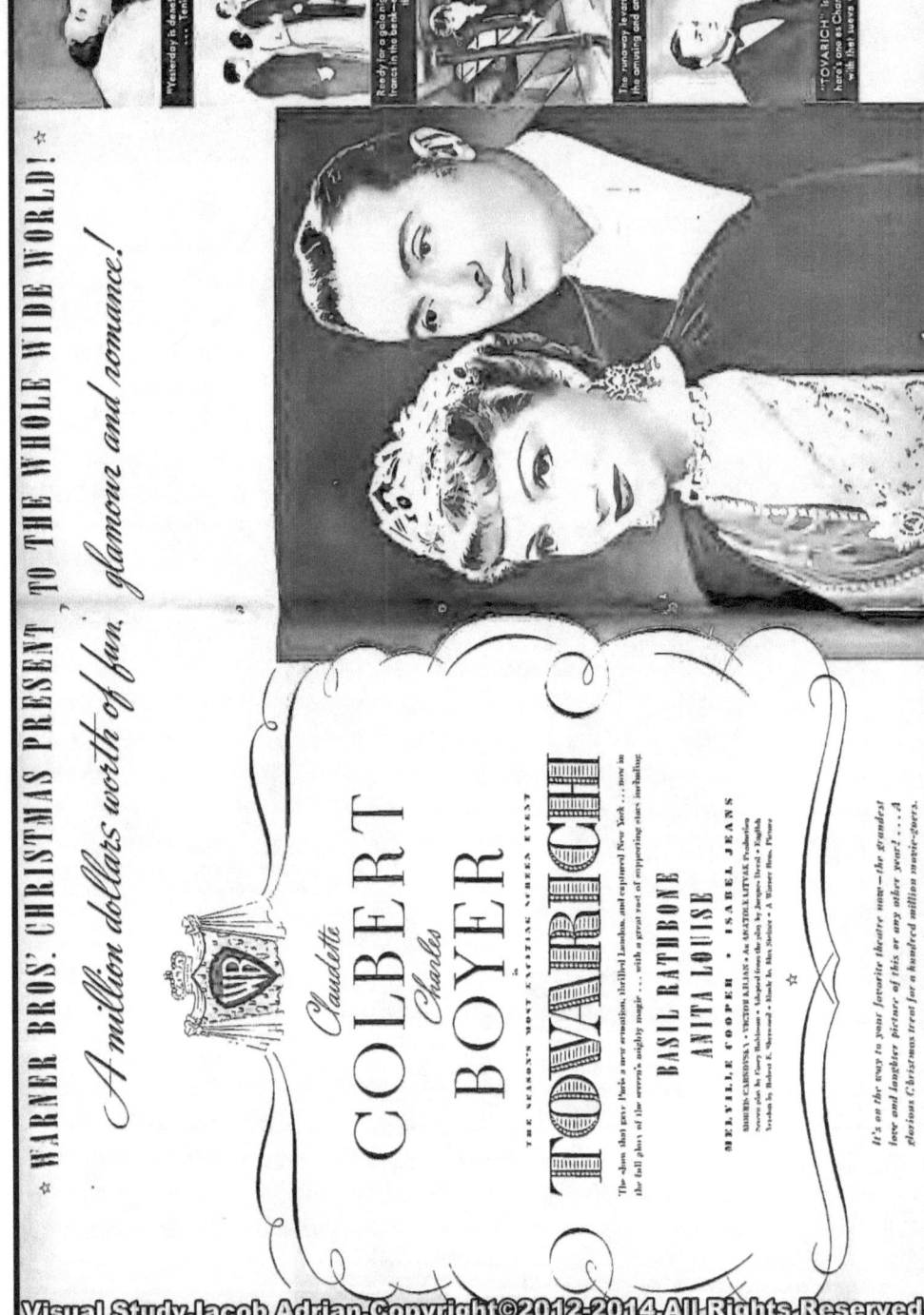

"He thought he knew how to tame a Frau, But Gary's in the Doghouse now... YOU BET..." *Claudette*

THE DOG-HOUSE

AMERICA'S LEADING LOVE TEAM IN THE COMEDY HIT OF 1938!

Adolph Zukor presents

CLAUDETTE COLBERT · GARY COOPER
"BLUEBEARD'S EIGHTH WIFE"

EDWARD EVERETT HORTON · DAVID NIVEN · ELIZABETH PATTERSON · HERMAN BING
Screen Play by Charles Brackett and Billy Wilder · A Paramount Picture
Based on the Play by Alfred Savoir · English Play Adaptation by Charlton Andrews

Produced and Directed by **ERNST LUBITSCH**

Laugh It Off

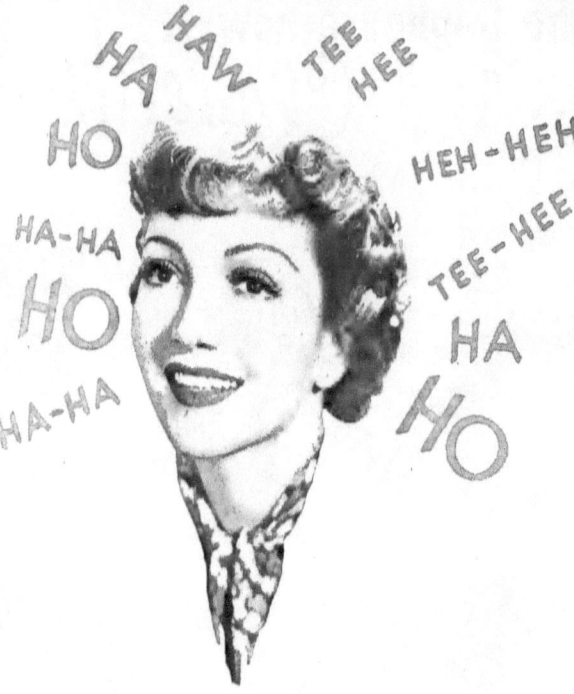

When you are happy, it does no harm to shed a few tears, thinks Claudette Colbert . . . . . but it is fatal to weep when things go wrong

By

E D G A R   B I R D M A N

■ The banquet was very elaborate, very formal, very social.

It was one of those tremendous things which happen in Hollywood every year or so. Producers and stars had assembled to do honor to the ambassador of one of the greatest nations in the world. Among those who graced the gallant occasion was Claudette Colbert—that stunning girl in white up there, sitting between the ambassador and one of the leading motion picture producers.

Claudette was feeling it—and how! She, like the banquet, was perfectly assembled. Her white dress was a creation of crepe, fresh from the salon of one of the better designers.

Far in the distance, away from the table at which sat Claudette and the other honored ones, sat another star. That star waved to Claudette, the wave clearly indicating:

"So you're up among the big shots."

Claudette gave a very languid, very broad A bow, and returned to the business of dissecting a chicken rich in brown gravy. The knife slipped, the chicken did a nip-up trailed by a tail of gravy and the ensemble lit in Claudette's lap.

For one horrible moment she sat, paralyzed.

"This is quite beyond everything," she told herself. "Shall I scream, cry, get up and run like everything, or just sit?"

She looked at the ambassador. The ambassador looked at her.

"Lively little thing, isn't it?" she asked.

The ambassador laughed. She laughed. She, the ambassador and waiters made repairs. The banquet went on its gallant way. Claudette told me today:

"That laugh saved the day for me. It was a laugh directed at myself. If you can't laugh at yourself you're in a very

bad way. I found it easy to do so, simply by comparing the Claudette of much dignity with the Claudette who played involuntary host to the chicken. I very quickly saw the line which divided a very impressive dignity from a person who looked very silly, and the line was so thin it wasn't at all important."

And she confessed:

"A few years ago, I'd have run from the banquet in confusion and would have had a good cry. That would have made things very uncomfortable for those around me as well as for myself."

The beneficial effects of a good guffaw have been proved to the star on many occasions. Recently she was discussing her work in a photoplay with a British critic.

"The picture wasn't very well received in England," the critic said. "The general concensus was that it could have been better."

Claudette sighed.

"Yes, indeed," she replied. "The American critics said that the plot wasn't all that it should have been."

■ Claudette was quite pleased with her work in that picture, and it was true that American critics had blamed story structure for the fact that it, while profitable, had not been a smash hit.

"It wasn't the story," said the critic. "It was your acting."

That was one time when Claudette had a hard time laughing it off, but she did. And she's glad she did. Because the critic left her thinking she was a very swell person. When you can laugh at criticism like that, you aren't in danger of snapping any hat bands.

■ Then there was that time at the opening of "See Naples And Die," Claudette's second or third big hit on the stage. She was feeling quite pleased with her ability as an actress. The critics were all set for a big moment in their lives when she walked onto the stage for her first entrance.

They got it.

Claudette tripped and fell flat on her face. She laughed that off, too, instead of retiring in confusion, and the audience liked her for it.

"Playing in comedies has since taught me to become used to being laughed at," she told me, as she walked out of a funny scene in Paramount's *Bluebeard's Eighth Wife*. "Nobody ever laughs at the straight man in a comedy scene because nothing silly ever happens to him. But they do laugh at the comedian, who is the butt of the jokes, and they go away remembering the comedian. He's the one who has given them a good time.

"It never hurts to be laughed at, on the screen or in real life—providing one laughs, too. The person who can't laugh, when victim of ego-shattering circumstances, is the one who is remembered as a poor sport."

■ Claudette has found, too, that the times when she has to laugh, and the laughs come

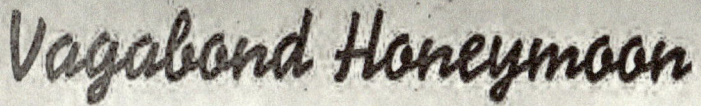

Vagabond Honeymoon

When a movie star determines to get away from the glamour of her career, it really can be done, and Claudette Colbert proved it

By HELEN BUNCH

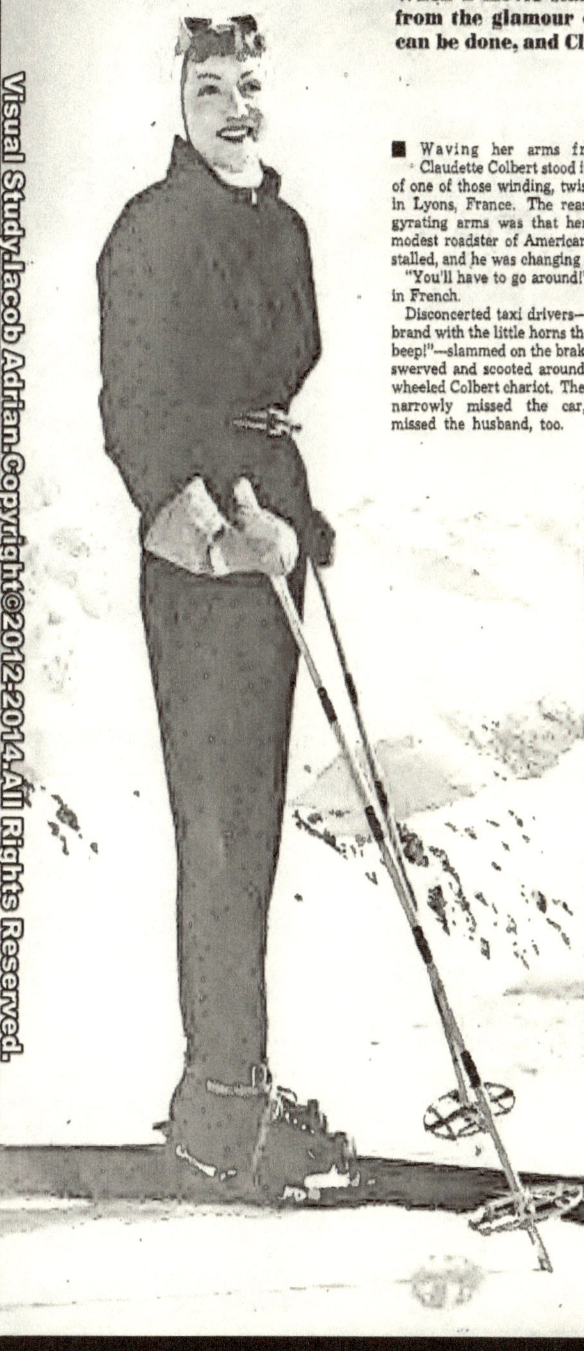

Waving her arms frantically, Claudette Colbert stood in the center of one of those winding, twisting streets in Lyons, France. The reason for the gyrating arms was that her husband's modest roadster of American make was stalled, and he was changing a tire.

"You'll have to go around!" she yelled in French.

Disconcerted taxi drivers—the French brand with the little horns that go "beep, beep!"—slammed on the brakes, skidded, swerved and scooted around the three-wheeled Colbert chariot. They grimaced, narrowly missed the car, narrowly missed the husband, too.

Not one guessed that they were making snide French cracks at the beautiful American motion picture star. For the simple reason that Miss Colbert was thoroughly incognito. She and her husband were wandering modestly about France, her native land, without trappings, without ballyhoo, and without giving much of a hang about doing anything but enjoying themselves.

They did that as "Mr. and Mrs. Jack Pressman".

"I wanted to show Jack what France was like and wanted to do it in peace," Claudette told me today. "Eight years ago, when I [Continued on page 55]

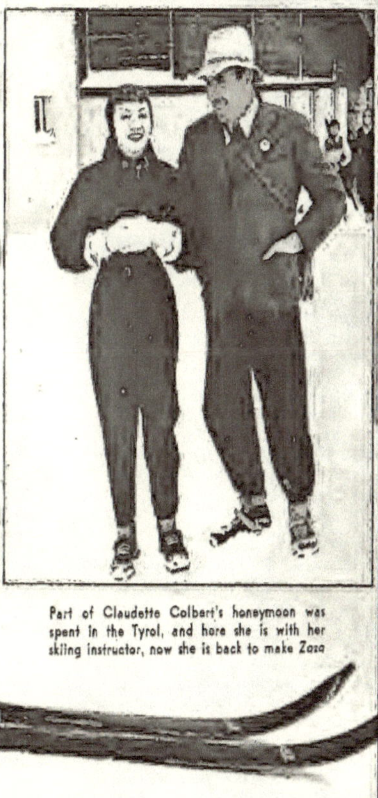

Part of Claudette Colbert's honeymoon was spent in the Tyrol, and here she is with her skiing instructor, now she is back to make Zaza

Vagabond Honeymoon

had no money, I toured the country very modestly—and had fun.

"This time, I thought at first Jack and I should do it with real style, and soon found out my mistake. I started off from Hollywood as a very fine lady. I had my maid, Therese Frank, my identity, and everything.

"Jack and I were going to have a delightfully formal time on our long planned honeymoon. We'd been married a year and a half and we'd never had it. So we swept through Paris and were off to play at San Moritz and St. Anton, two winter sports spots, one in Switzerland, the other in the Austrian Tyrol.

"For a while it was fun, but after the first thrill of skiing wore off, the candid cameras, newspaper people, formal functions, and very, very social receptions became too much the Hollywood pattern. We resolved to be informal."

The informality was a lot of fun. The trip was conducted on such a modest basis that before Claudette and her husband had seen everything they wanted, she was down to doing her own washing!

Claudette came home showing the benefit of being absolutely herself. She has a calm serenity, a lack of nerves, a natural buoyancy which she hasn't had for years—and several of those years have been dropped by the wayside, as well.

"We spent a month forgetting about work and who we were and who we were supposed to be," Claudette said. "I promised Jack I'd show him the countryside and I did. I discovered parts of it I never knew existed. It was glorious! I was tired after it was over, but it was the kind of tired feeling you enjoy."

Claudette laughed.

■ "The informal trip happened a bit by accident," she said. "After we left San Moritz and the Tyrol we came back to Paris at loose ends. We faced a lot of rushing around. One night I told Jack what I thought we ought to do and he agreed on the spur of the moment. We put Terry, the maid, all my finery in a Paris hotel. Jack got a drive-yourself car. And away we went."

Claudette was humming happily as the car rolled into the Parisian suburbs. In her hand was a guide book published by a tire manufacturing firm. In the back of the roadster were her two bags and one which belonged to her husband. It was the romantic month of April, when the woods were just beginning to turn green and the orchards were just beginning to bud. Romance?

"We found it at every turn in the road," she said. "Quaint peasants in old-world costumes. Wagons, carts and horses and little one-way roads. And the guidebook was a peach! We arranged our tour so that we stopped at odd little places where the food was good for lunch, took time to walk through the provincial towns. Nights we planned to stop at cities which at least boasted of hotels which had rooms with baths. We covered about one hundred and fifty miles a day, just loafing along."

There were no praise agents, ballyhoo artists and advance notices within hundreds of miles.

■ "But I very nearly got caught up with in one town," Claudette revealed. "Nobody had been paying any attention to us. We'd registered under my husband's name. In this particular hotel, we followed the same routine. We had the bags brought in, registered, and Jack went out to put the car in a nearby garage.

"When Jack returned to the lobby, the clerk said:

"'Pardon me, sir—but your wife bears remarkable resemblance to an American film player named Colbert—Claudette Colbert.'

"'Yes, indeed—' Jack assured him. 'We've been told that before.'

"He hurried upstairs to tell me. We were worried lest the village turn out, and everybody'd get very formal. Anything but that! We noticed that we were eyed warily when we went to dinner. We retired, and the next morning prepared to leave bright and early. Jack brought the car to the door. I was just about to leave when the clerk, who was again on duty, asked me:

"'Will the madame please sign the special guest register?'

"I saw a suspicious twinkle in his eye. So I signed 'Claudette Colbert' and then beat a hurried retreat. The word sped like wildfire and by the time I got into the car heads were sticking out of windows."

■ The hours of travel were long and each day was full. Claudette didn't want to waste any of the precious time. They rose at seven. They dressed hurriedly for the next adventure. They breakfasted. And then they were off to explore new worlds.

"One of the biggest thrills," Claudette related, "was when we were travelling through the 'castle country.' We saw one chateau which particularly intrigued us. It was gaunt, and forbidding, and the walls had wasted away through the years. It sent a shudder down my spine and I discovered that Jack got the same reaction.

"We decided that such a place must hold a large assortment of sinister secrets and investigated. We found out that a bloodthirsty gentleman named Gil de Retz, the original 'bluebeard' of history, had erected it. This was an odd coincidence, after I'd just finished making *Bluebeard's Eighth Wife*, which wasn't a bit sinister, but sounded so."

At another tiny village, where the peasants wore lace caps and full skirts and wooden shoes, Claudette discovered an antique shop which was filled with treasures. She explored it, found that the proprietor wasn't there. She left her Paris address, explaining:

"There are several things I would like to have."

She pointed them out, gave her husband's name.

"And the antique dealer apparently wasn't at all impressed, because I never

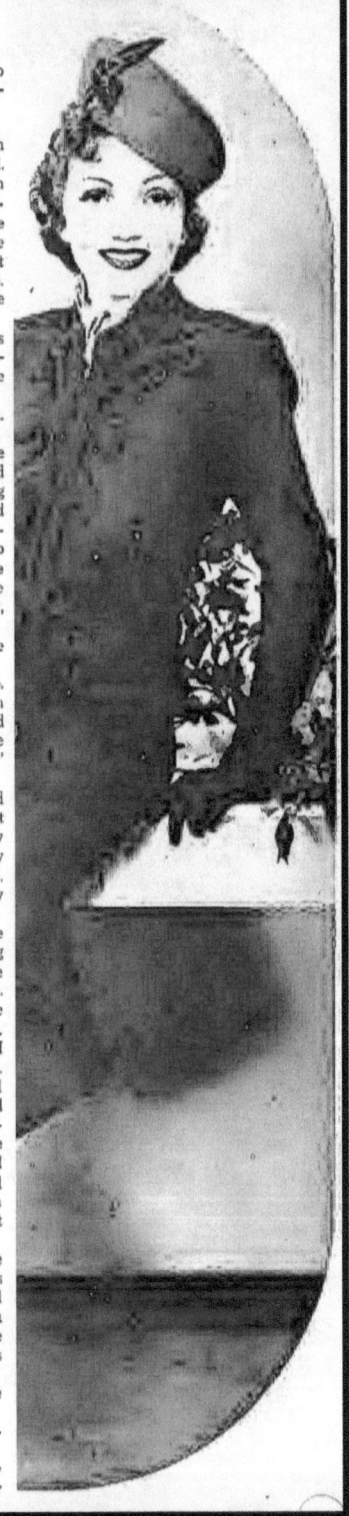

heard from him," she concluded. "I'm glad—it proves I was just another tourist."

■ "One strange way that I preserved my incognito," she explained, "was to speak English. The French people, some of whom suspected that I was an actress, were completely disarmed by this language. Odd? Not at all. You see, they are used to seeing me in American pictures onto which French voices have been dubbed. They believe that Claudette speaks French all the time!"

Had Claudette, feeling like a child out of school, suddenly decided to go formal, there would have been big turnouts, especially in the larger cities.

"American films play there, all with the French dubbing, as I've explained," she said. "In fact, one of the biggest laughs of the trip came when we decided to sneak into a picture show just to see what it would be like. It was a typical 'cops and robbers' affair, with Jimmy Cagney, Frank McHugh and Pat O'Brien in the cast. When we heard Jimmy lisp—'Oui, maman' —it was too much for us. The idea of Jimmy talking that way sent us into hysterics. The French audience, outraged, turned and stared at us as if we were crazy."

■ Claudette made one concession to her profession. She carried her camera with her. And she snapped pictures as the merry tour took them to and through quaint Brittany, along the chateaus of the lovely, winding Loire, down to the Pyrenees, grim and forbidding, to Biarritz, to old fort at Carcassonne, to Nîmes and Arles in the old Roman country. Each day of travel became more enchanting.

On the winding, carefree journey they stopped at the little village of Le Blanc. Parenthetically, it was at this time that Claudette, fresh out of make-up and fresh out of stockings, took to washing them out and hanging them up to dry in the modest rooms which they had engaged, even as you and I! LeBlanc was doubly interesting for it was here that Claudette's grandfather lived, and here that she spent her summers as a child.

"It was amazing to approach that quaint town and see it unfold just as my memory had pictured it for so long," she said. "You see, I left there when I was just seven. I thought that memory would have been mistaken. But when we started sloping down toward the river, I told Jack:

" 'To get to grandfather's house, you cross the bridge and turn up the first street to the left.'

"I pointed out a certain house. Jack stopped the car. I got out. It was a fresh, sunny, Easter morning. Two old men approached us, shuffling over the broken pavement. In French, I asked them if the house had not once been owned by the family Chauchoin.

" 'Yes,' one replied. 'Old Chauchoin had a son, George, who went to America to find his fortune, taking his family.'

" 'Why, that was my father!' I exclaimed. After this identification, the old fellow told me many fascinating, half-remembered things. As he talked I noted the house no longer had a balcony. It had not

been replaced since the day it had caved in with me while I stood on it watching a parade pass."

■ Days drifted by, and finally Claudette found herself on the Riviera, in Southern France, just beginning to warm beneath the benign spring sun. After that, Marseilles for bouillabaisse, which Claudette had promised would be a treat. It was. Then back through the Dauphine province to Paris—through Grenoble, along the road of Napoleon.

Paris in May.

■ For a month, Claudette and her husband slipped into their old routine, "did the town." She had met the Duke of Kent while skiing. Now she met the Duke of Windsor and his charming wife, the former Wallis Warfield Simpson.

"It was at a soiree given by the former Elsie De Wolfe, now Lady Mendl," she said. "The Duke was his gallant, yet quiet and unassuming self. To be perfectly frank, I didn't remind him of the time he came to America in 1918 and I, a New York school child, met him aboard the cruiser, the H. M. S. Renown. I represented the French school girl making good in America. To prove how good I was I wore a white, starched dress, waved an American flag and recited a blundering little speech. During the time that I spoke and the other little girl, who was a typical American making good in America, said her bit, he was quite bored, and I hardly blame him. I remember how he dug the scabbard of his sword into the toe of his boot, and I wanted to give up and run."

Claudette laughed at the memory.

"The Duchess of Windsor proved far more fascinating than I had imagined she would be," she continued. "She is not a tall woman and yet, because of her dignity and charm, she appears tall. She is beautifully groomed, beautifully dressed, reserved, and with a definitely winning personality. The photographs which we see in America don't treat her fairly. In real life, she is far more the woman you would expect her to be."

There were many other gay parties and formal events and receptions and functions. Claudette and her husband were gay in their rounds, quite formal and polite.

"And," Claudette confesses, "I found myself looking back on our vagabond jaunt as the thrill of the trip and the thrill of my life. Usually, when one goes back to recapture things which in retrospect seem beautiful, they disappoint. This time it was just the opposite. My husband found my country beautiful, interesting, even fascinating. To me, it enriched the present as well as brightened fading memories.

Coming back through the customs to America, Claudette had nothing of great value to declare—just a few French garments which she hadn't been able to resist.

"The things of value which I brought back," she told me, "are not the kind one declares at customs. They're locked in my heart."

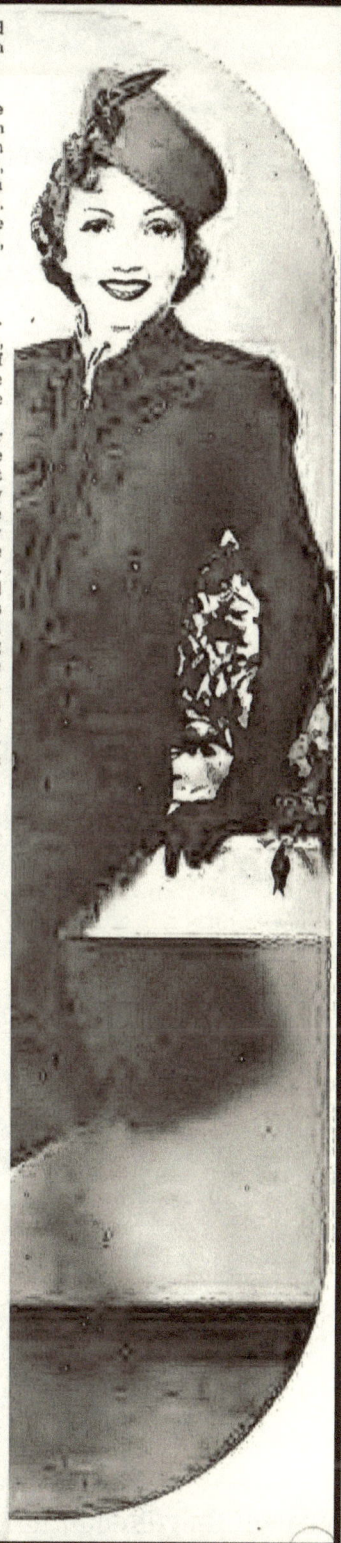

CLAUDETTE COLBERT n

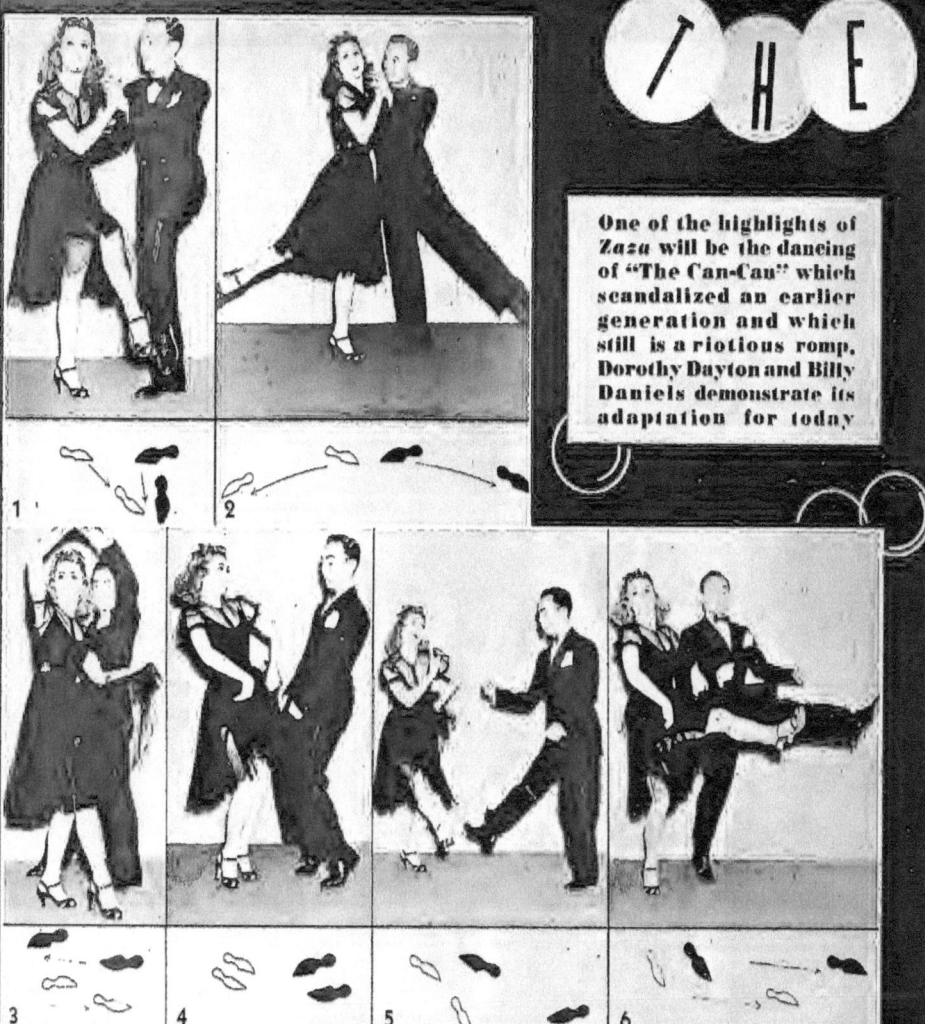

One of the highlights of *Zaza* will be the dancing of "The Can-Can" which scandalized an earlier generation and which still is a riotious romp. Dorothy Dayton and Billy Daniels demonstrate its adaptation for today

1 Here is the first position in the new swing swagger . . . Hop eight beats on one foot, swinging the other

2 The hop step is continued for another eight beats, but notice the new positions of the swinging feet

3 Partners change sides on a two step for four counts, return to first position, repeat the "Can-Can Hop"

4 Partners circle each other, Billy imitating Dorothy's "swish" with a vigorous hop, then they do the . . .

5 "Slap it" in which both dancers hop left, slapping right foot, alternating this step for eight counts

6 For the "Cake Walk" Dorothy and Billy swing back to center on four counts and face center for . . .

7 "The Can-Can Walk." Both partners hop on left foot, crossing right foot over for four counts, and repeat

8 After a jump into the air, Dorothy and Billy show, energetically, how to do "The Break" after which . . .

9 Dorothy circles, extending right foot. Billy does "The Brush-off," dusting her shoe for eight beats

10 The partners swing back to back, heels together, in their original position. Continue till exhausted!

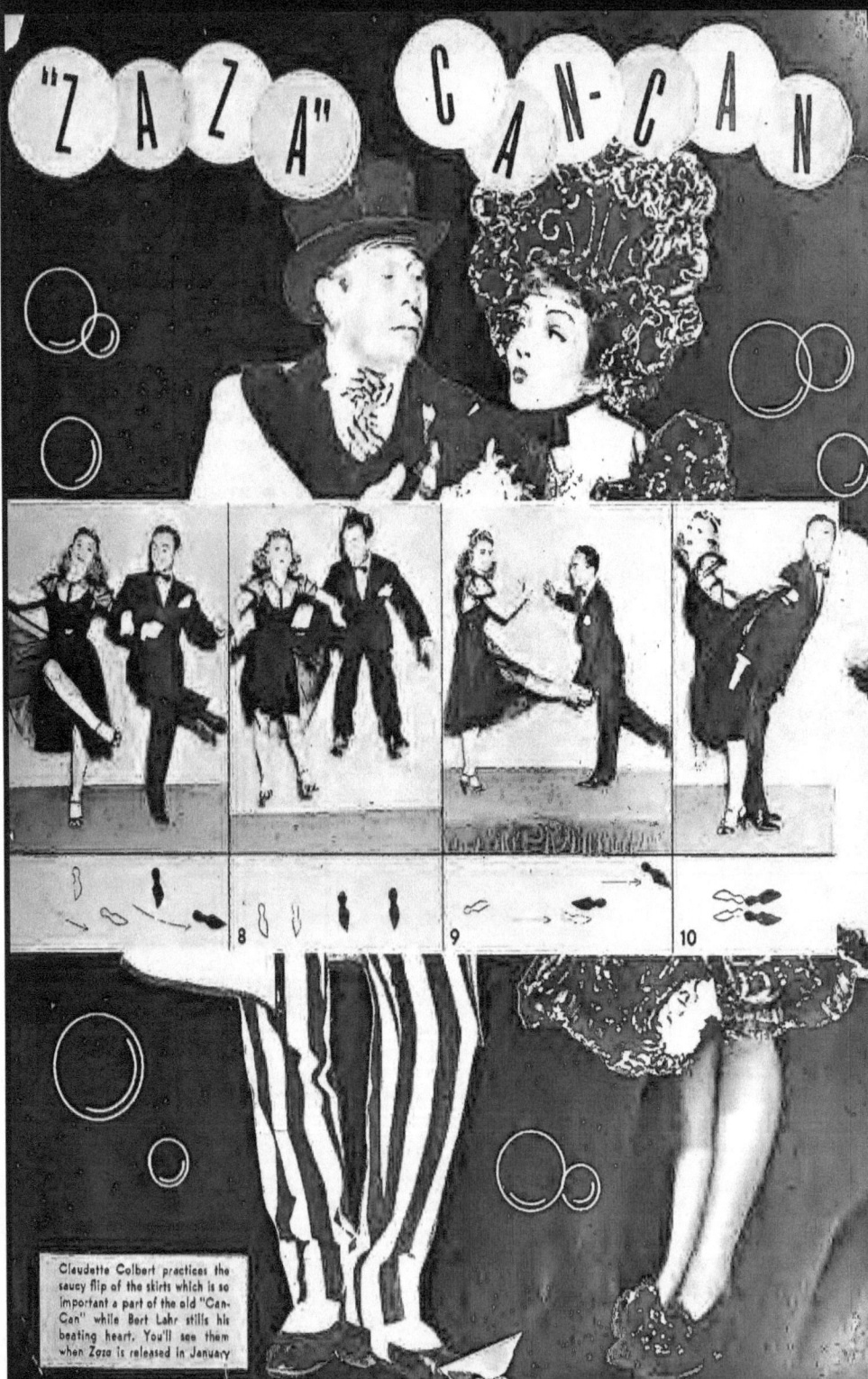

"ZAZA" CAN-CAN

Claudette Colbert practices the saucy flip of the skirts which is so important a part of the old "Can-Can" while Bert Lahr stills his beating heart. You'll see them when Zaza is released in January

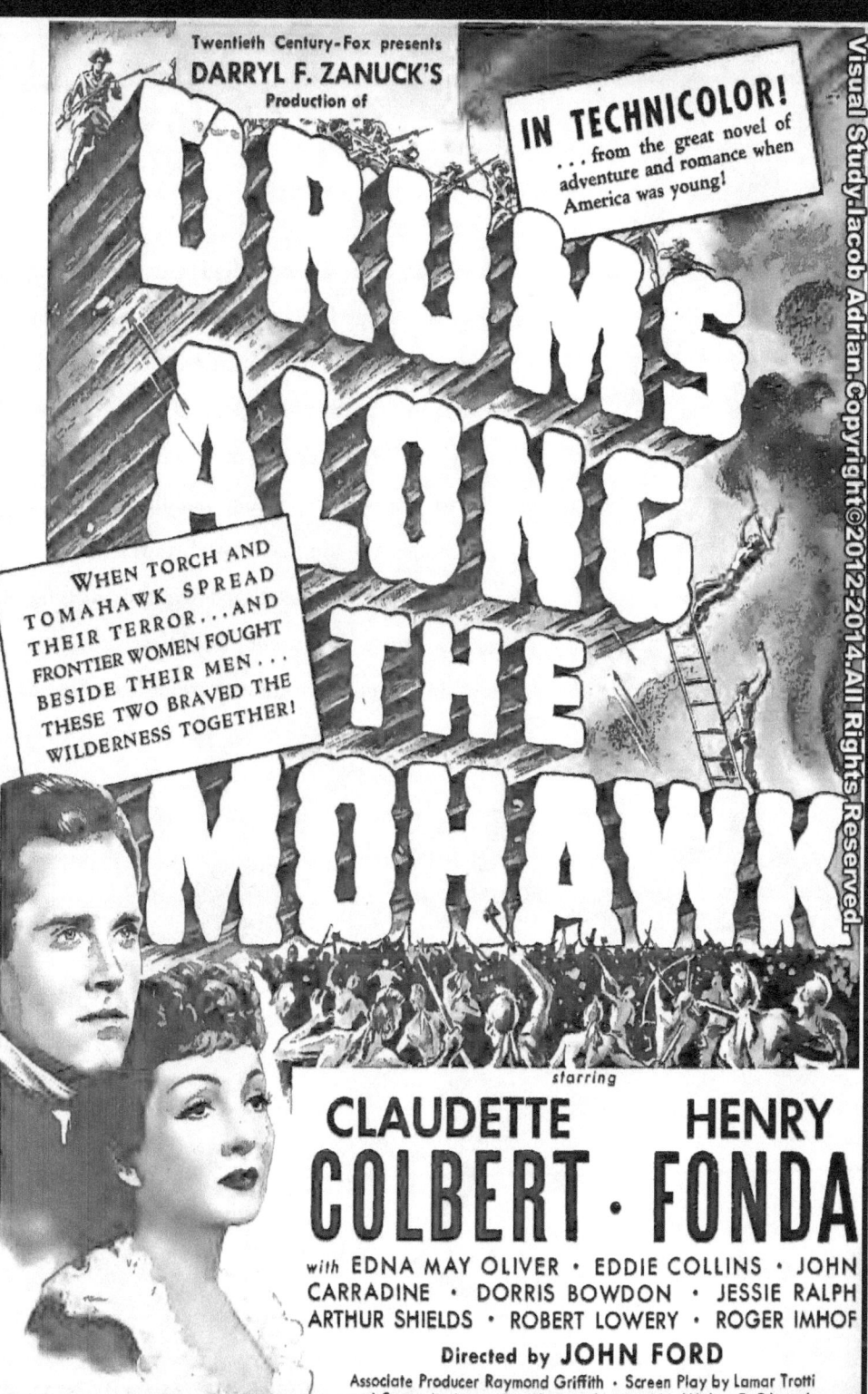

"I love you

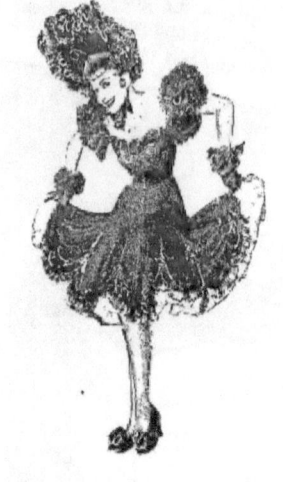

Words torn from the anguished heart of a woman in love ... words breathing the intense emotion of a proud woman whose pride has vanished in the wonder, the thrilling glory of her first great love ... the words of the immortal Zaza to her beloved Bernard ... pouring tumultuously from the screen as Claudette Colbert brings Zaza, gay, reckless Zaza, who loved too well, to thrilling, glorious life in Claudette's mightiest acting triumph, in the year's grandest screen love drama.

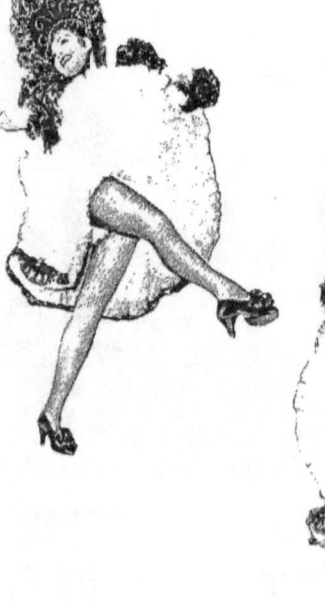

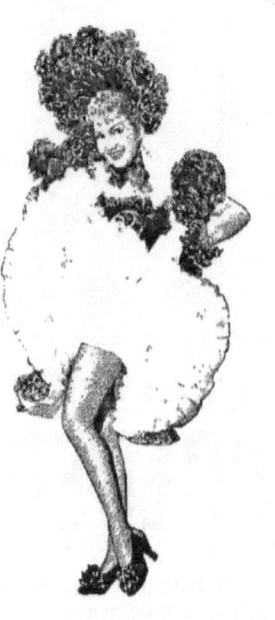

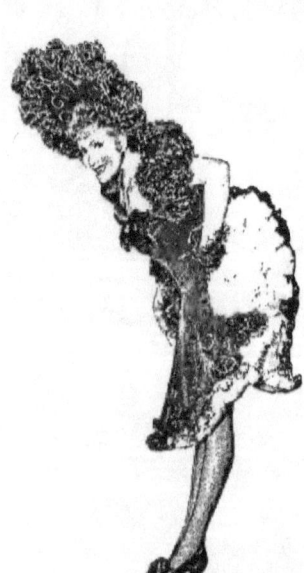

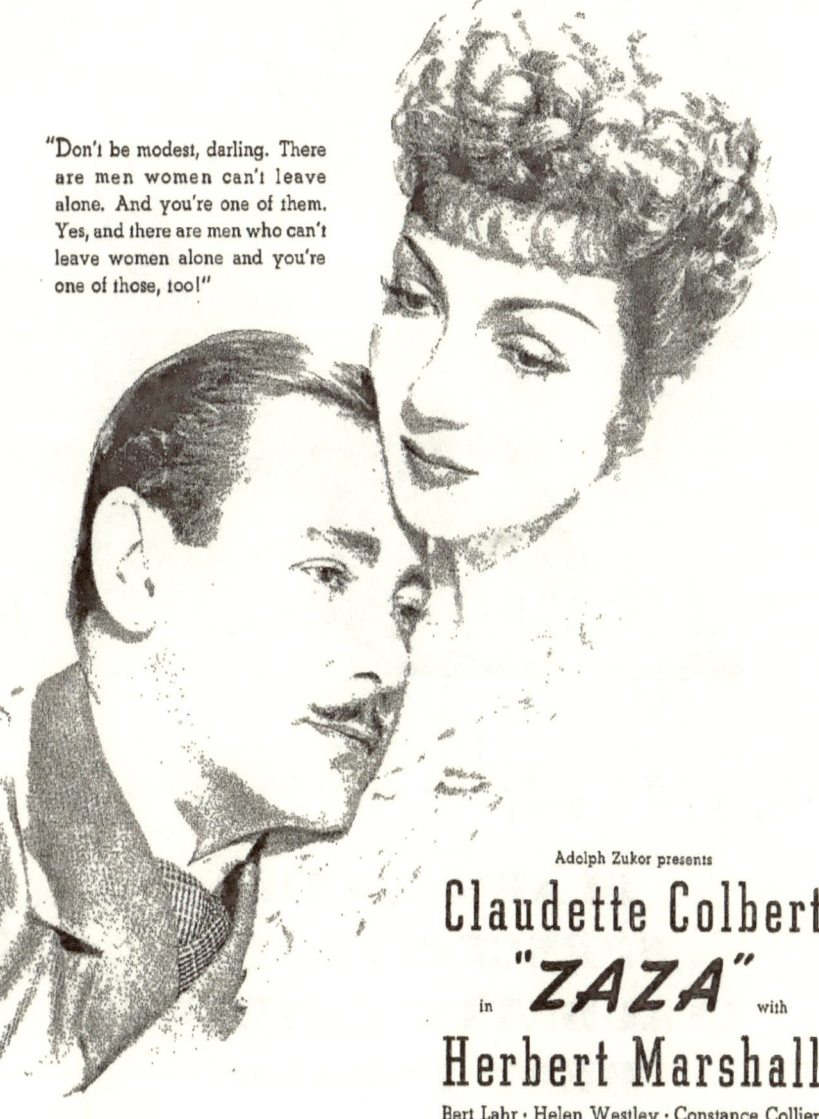

more than you love me . . ."

"Don't be modest, darling. There
are men women can't leave
alone. And you're one of them.
Yes, and there are men who can't
leave women alone and you're
one of those, too!"

Adolph Zukor presents

Claudette Colbert
in *"ZAZA"* with
Herbert Marshall

Bert Lahr · Helen Westley · Constance Collier
Genevieve Tobin · Walter Catlett
Directed by George Cukor · Produced by Albert Lewin
Screen Play by Zoe Akins · From the Play by Pierre Berton & Charles Simon
A Paramount Picture

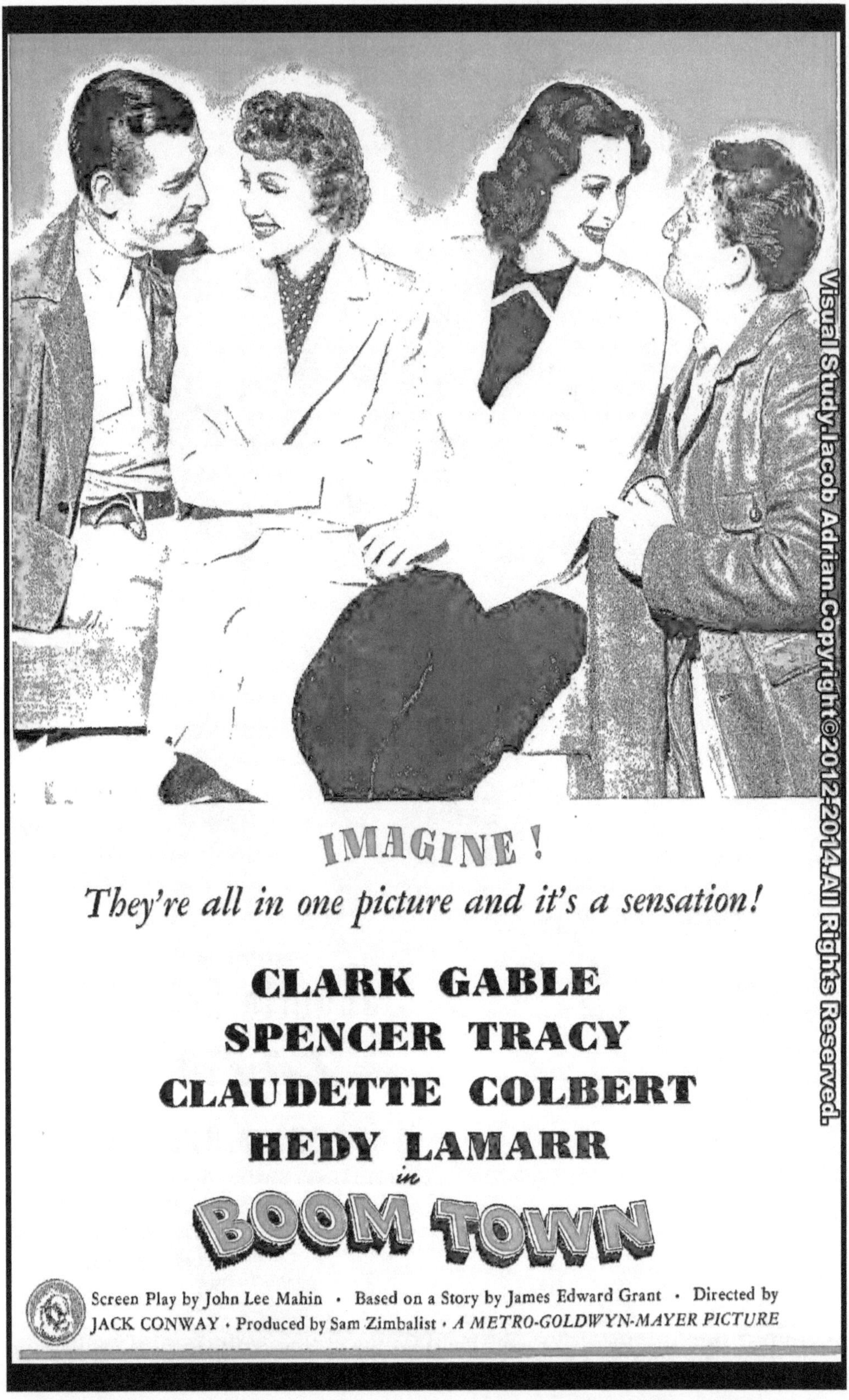

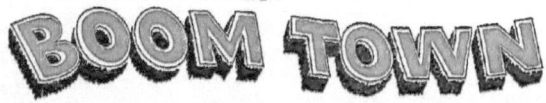

IMAGINE !

They're all in one picture and it's a sensation!

CLARK GABLE
SPENCER TRACY
CLAUDETTE COLBERT
HEDY LAMARR

in

BOOM TOWN

 Screen Play by John Lee Mahin · Based on a Story by James Edward Grant · Directed by
JACK CONWAY · Produced by Sam Zimbalist · *A METRO-GOLDWYN-MAYER PICTURE*

■ Claudette Colbert, *tres* glamorous in red lounging pajamas, had just received a lingering kiss from Ray Milland on the set of *Skylark*. She turned to me and said, "That's the sort of thing that makes a girl feel feminine all over again.

"I've never felt better cast," she added, with a gleam in those brown eyes. "In real life, too, as in this new picture, I practically drive my husband crazy with the things I take it into my head to do."

Was she kidding?

"No, indeed, I'm not kidding," said Claudette, shaking her head. "I'm a case for a psycho-analyst. I'm forever finding myself doing something I never expected to do—all because I obeyed an impulse.

"I don't know whether that's the French in me coming out, or what. There's an old French saying, 'The first thought you have was sent from heaven above. Follow it—it's for you.'

"Or maybe, subconsciously, I'd like to believe that old myth that a girl's best friend is her instinct. If feminine intuition really paid off, life would be simple.

"So I make life difficult for myself and obey impulses.

"When I was a youngster, I was determined to be a ballet dancer. The best ballet dancer in the world. Another Pavlova. But one little impulse was the finish of that.

"We lived in a flat in New York. One day I was out in front, bouncing a ball against the wall of the building. The ball went in the street. I dashed after it—without looking or thinking. I was in the street before I saw the truck coming. I screamed, and then fainted. I don't remember actually being hit. The next I knew, I was in a hospital bed, in agony—bruised from head to foot. And with one leg broken in about three places. I spent four months in bed. I finally gave up my dream of ever being a dancer.

"Another little impulse was the finish of my father's ambition for me. He wanted me to be a singer. He was convinced that I had a voice worth developing. But we never found out for sure because, one day after school, I had the urge to go ice-skating, even though I wasn't dressed for it. As an aftermath of that little urge, I came down with the world's worst case of laryngitis—which left me with a chronic hoarseness that I didn't outgrow for years.

"After a couple of catastrophes like that, you'd think I would have been cured of ever being impulsive again. But no."

Everybody has had the urge to go around the world on a tramp freighter —but Claudette's the girl who obeyed that impulse.

"I decided to go, just like that." She snapped her fingers. "It was a wonderful trip, and I've never regretted taking it.

"Every trip I've ever made, I've made on an impulse. I'm superstitious about planning trips. So many things can happen to spoil plans. I'm sure it's more fun, just setting out when the urge strikes

you—the way my husband and I did three years ago, when we went to Europe.

"When we were married, we had only a week for a honeymoon so we went to Yosemite. While there, we took up skiing. We had just enough of it to tantalize us. All the next year, we kept talking about how we were really going to learn how to ski. Until finally I said, 'If we're going to learn how, let's learn from experts. Let's go to the Tyrol.' So we took three months off and went to the Tyrol."

Now, every chance they get, they obey the urge to go to Sun Valley. Claudette even won a slalom race there last winter.

"I didn't plan to enter. I had never slalomed in my life. At the last minute, somebody said, 'Go on, try it.' And, suddenly, I found myself at the starting line, shaking from head to foot. Only a moment before, I had been positively healthy, and so happy. . . . I still don't know how I won the race.

"I'm forever getting in difficulties, obeying that impulse to do as the natives do. I'll never forget one time in Bali, when I went out by myself at night to watch a native ceremony. It wasn't exactly voodoo, but it was something akin to it. I had heard that they ate fire. They hypnotized themselves into chewing live coals. But nobody had told me that, at a certain point in the proceedings, a big dragon made of water buffalo hide would appear on the scene. This thing suddenly came leaping out. I was so surprised that I sat down on the ground. And, as I sat, I landed on a toad." Claudette shuddered in reminiscence. "I'm telling you my scream scared the natives right out of their trances."

Claudette hates hats, and never wears

one if she can avoid it. Yet if she feels miserable or at a loss, she buys a hat.

"I often think of that line Mary Boland had in *Three-Cornered Moon* when she learned she was penniless. 'But what did you do, Mama?' her brood asked. She said, 'What *could* I do? I went to the beauty shop and had my hair washed' . . . I know exactly how she felt. Though probably my impulse has less sense than hers, because I haven't any use for hats.

"You can quote me as saying that, in general, it isn't smart to be impulsive, but it's fun. If I were qualified to hand out any advice on the subject of impulse, I'd say, 'Give it a second thought!'"

END

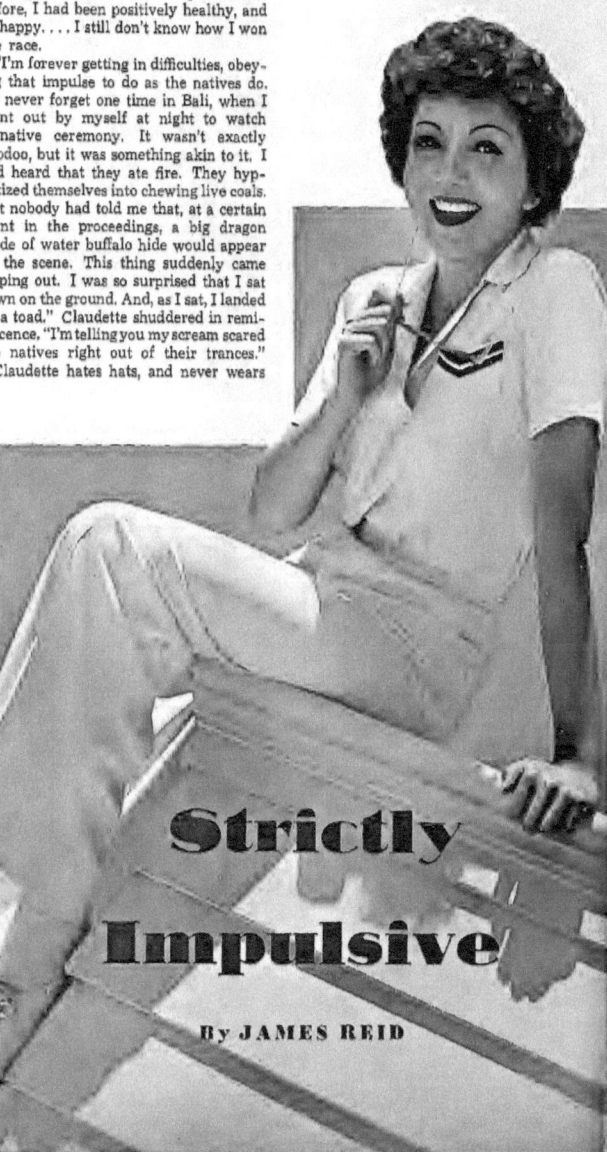

Strictly
Impulsive

By JAMES REID

Claudette Colbert repeats a lucky impulse by again requesting Ray Milland as her leading man for Paramount's new film, *Skylark*

Tough Orchid

By HELEN LOUISE WALKER

Everyone gets so puzzled about Claudette Colbert. And it is a rather curious thing when you come to think of it. For years her sheer exquisiteness has been a sort of Hollywood legend. Until you've lunched with Claudette from one of those fabulous hampers which arrive at her studio dressing room every day, you simply haven't seen anything. If you've dined at her home you know something about Continental living at its finest. Her house and her clothes, her silken sheets and convent-made underwear are things the Hollywood gossips discuss with an odd sort of pride. These same gossips point to her with emphasis when snooty visitors accuse the colony of being gauche or vulgar.

One of these boasters was proclaiming, "Most Hollywood people live well. Claudette lives delicately. But she is so fragile . . ."

Cecil de Mille happened to overhear and he roared with laughter. "Fragile! That one?" he chortled. "Why, she can take more physical punishment than Tarzan. I know!" And he launched into a lusty description of the first picture he made with Claudette. The cast and crew of *Four Frightened People* went to the Hawaiian Islands on location. Not to a big resort hotel mind you. But to one of the islands where there isn't much except jungles and large bugs and lizards and mud. Claudette had just had a serious operation. She was so ill, indeed, that the company sailed for the Islands without her and she went to the harbor in an ambulance to catch the next ship, completing her convalescence on the way across. She had fought for the chance to go and go she did, in spite of hell and high water and a barely healed incision! De Mille relates that on the day she

arrived she had to go into the surf and take a pounding from the waves which were not nearly as gentle as the travel folders may have led you to believe. After that the company moved to an inland location to which they had to travel every morning, over rough country, on mule-back. And here the script called for Claudette to prance about and try to look happy under an icy waterfall. This presented some difficulty because the impact of the water made her gasp and she spoiled a couple of takes by sputtering.

"I laughed at her," C. B. relates, with relish. "And finally she got so mad that she reached out, grabbed my sleeve, caught me off balance and pulled me into the cold torrent with her. It made me gasp, too, and I was wearing a good many more clothes than she was. This little revenge made her feel better and she finished the scene with no more gasping. Fragile? Hah!"

That's what they said when she was playing in *Boom Town* and took her drenching with mud and oil, helped fight the oil well fire, and bent over that steaming wash tub.

It wouldn't seem quite so outrageous if you hadn't seen her at home. That bedroom . . . all peach satin and point d'esprit ruffles. Lace over satin. Petticoats on the bed and on the mirrored dressing table in its windowed recess. Crystal bottles, embroidered cushions piled about, an occasional blue satin bow somewhere, just for fun. Claudette has let frivolity run away with her in her own room. It's fluffy and gay and feminine.

The rest of her Georgian house has dignity and simplicity. Correct period furniture in the living room. The dining room is formal to the point of stateliness. The playroom (which is also a projection

room) is ample and designed for fun.

But—watch Claudette presiding at one of her so-carefully-thought-out small dinner parties. Then think of her in that scene in *Skylark* where she tumbled down the stairs to the galley of the little boat where she made, spilled and re-made the coffee. Remember?

That shot wasn't made on location. It was made in a tank at the studio where the storm stirred up was a good deal more violent than a real storm encountered on angry days in the Pacific. But the studio-made storm, violent as it was, didn't photograph to the director's satisfaction. Claudette stumbled, slipped and fell down those stairs *ten times* before everything lunged and swayed for a proper take. She bruised her elbows and her knees and the part of the anatomy which usually suffers when one falls downstairs. When she was finished and they patched her up, she had enough iodine and adhesive tape decorating her pretty chassis to stock a small hospital. But she was cheerful as all get-out.

It's not that she never complains, that she is a "martyr to her art" or any such nonsense. She values her skin and hates a broken leg as much as you do. One director said of her, "There's one nice thing about Claudette. If she's going to do any beefing about a scene, she does it *beforehand*. She gives you that horrified little squeal, 'Oooooh, do I HAVE to do that?' Once she's convinced that the scene belongs in the picture, she makes a face and says, 'O. K.' and that's all there is to it. From there on in she doesn't pull her punches.

She was almost as frail as she looks when she first came to Hollywood. She was constantly struggling to put on weight. She says that isn't true any more. She thinks she started to improve in health and general stamina when she stopped pampering herself. If Hollywood still thinks of her as a fragile creature, she thinks that is very amusing.

"I have," she says, firmly, "the appetite and the nervous system of a truck driver."

How did she achieve this enviable state? "Well-ll, I discovered that to do a good job in anything you had to go all the way. I mean, you had to do things *hard* or they didn't register. You had to be thorough. Then I began to discover that a lot of other things in life were more fun if you were thorough about them, too. If you 'go all out' for things, you get more out of them—or is this getting scrambled?"

She discovered, for instance, that exercise was fun and not a duty. She plays a good game of tennis and likes to swim but she didn't discover her real passion until she went to Sun Valley for *She Met Him in Paris* and discovered skiing. She twisted her ankle that time and had to finish the picture with a tightly taped stem. But on her next vacation she learned to swoop and skim with the best of them.

"Yes, I learned to think things *hard*," Claudette continued. "Then I learned to do them that way. Fittings, photographs, falling downstairs, playing games, talking with people—everything. The more I did, the more I found I could do and the more fun it was. If anyone tells you that I'm an orchid, tell him for me that orchids are really hardy plants. They're tough!"

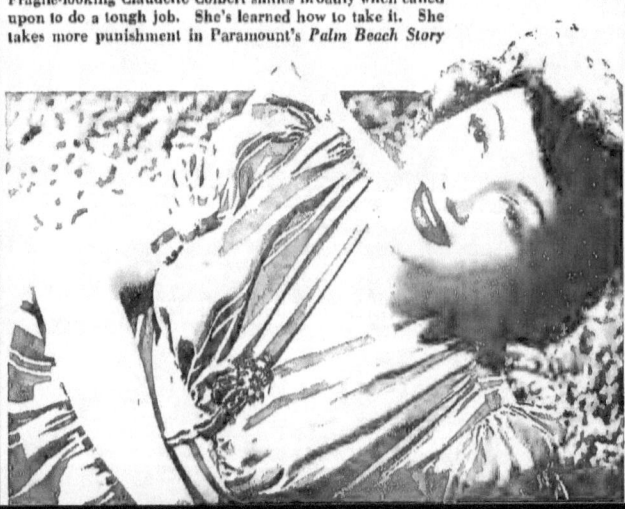

Fragile-looking Claudette Colbert smiles broadly when called upon to do a tough job. She's learned how to take it. She takes more punishment in Paramount's *Palm Beach Story*

Popping Questions at Claudette Colbert

Quizzed by HELEN HOVER

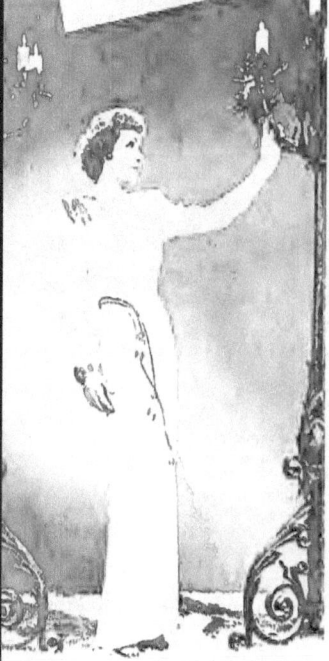

Claudette Colbert not only possesses one of Hollywood's loveliest figures, but a very rare sense of humor as well. She's in Paramount's *No Time for Love*

Claudette's home in Holmby Hills is a "gold brick"

Q. Why won't you allow your husband to be photographed with you?

A. It would hurt him in his profession —medicine—which does not approve of personal publicity for its members, and I consider his career much more important than mine. Unfortunately, some people have misunderstood our stand and think we're high-hat or snobbish to the press, but that's not so. I see no reason for my husband to jeopardize his standing in his profession just because my career invites so much publicity.

Q. What are your plans for being with your husband while he is in the service?

A. To spend every moment I possibly can with him. Only Hollywood contracts, which already obligate me, and war work will keep me from him.

Q. What are your plans when you retire from the screen?

A. I hope to direct or produce pictures—and I have an idea in back of my head that I'd like to coach youngsters.

Q. What is the funniest thing that ever happened to you?

A. In a scene one day for a picture, I was posed dramatically and languorously on a chaise lounge. I was never more elegant or "movie star-ish." Suddenly the legs of the lounge gave way and I found myself sprawled very un-languorously on the floor.

Q. Do you allow yourself to be photographed in bathing suits?

A. No. I think it is undignified—for me, that is, unless a scene in a picture calls for it. I am not opposed to bathing suit art in general, and think it fine for the newer crop of starlets. But not for me, thank you.

Q. Are you a good housekeeper?

A. You bet! I proudly admit that I can cook, sew, wash and iron.

Q. What do you consider the high point of your life?

A. The night I eloped with my husband.

Q. What do you like most about your work?

A. Having people in far places recognize me. I guess that's a hammy admission, but it's a great thrill and I'm grateful for it.

Q. What do you like least about your work?

A. Getting up at six every morning!

Q. Whom do you consider the five handsomest men in pictures?

A. Clark Gable, Tyrone Power, Ronald Colman, Errol Flynn and Cary Grant. But not in order. Don't pin me down as to who is handsomest of the five—puh-leeze!

Q. Why did you move back to your Holmby Hills house after a few months in a small apartment?

A. Frankly, no one wants to purchase or rent a large home in these times, and I don't like to have it remain empty.

Q. What are some of your eccentricities or fixed habits?

A. I like small parties. I don't use any nail polish. I stick to the same hair style, year in and year out. I stick to the same type of hat, no matter how styles change—the wide brimmed sailor.

Q. What childhood wish have you never realized and still hope to attain?

A. I have always wanted to christen a battleship—but so far I've never done it. I think that would be the crowning glory of my life.

Q. What was your most embarrassing moment?

A. If you ever had a half broiled chicken drop in your lap while lunching with the French Ambassador, you would never forget it. Neither have I! I tried to cut the chicken and the whole thing dived into my lap. My face was never redder. Why do things like that always happen when you're with a dignitary whom you want to impress?

Claudette's favorite feature: Her brown eyes. Can you blame her?

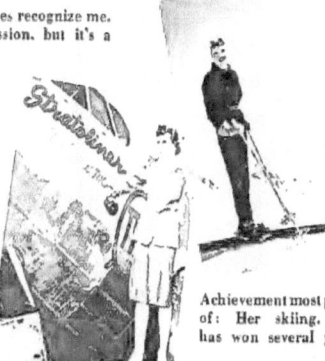

Achievement most proud of: Her skiing. She has won several prizes

She christened Stratoliner, now wants to christen a battleship

Q. What rumor upset you the most?

A. The constant rumors that Dr. Pressman and I were not happy together. Denying them would just add dignity to the reports, so we had to take it in silence.

Q. Do you think a girl with a husband or fiance in the service should go out with other men?

A. No, except occasionally with mutual friends and in groups.

Q. How do you occupy yourself while your husband is away in the service?

A. Work at the studio, camp tours and canteen activities. I'd be excruciatingly lonely if I had nothing to do while he was away.

Q. Who is your idea of the woman of the year?

A. Madame Chiang Kai-shek—

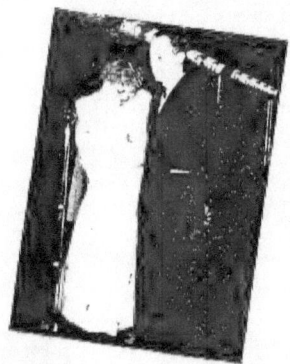

One of the few photos of Claudette and husband, Dr. Joel Pressman

for her supreme courage and the eternal hope that she has instilled in the hearts of her own countrymen and all free men throughout the world. I think she is one of the greatest women of all times.

Q. What is your pet beauty secret?

A. Soap and water.

Q. What is your pet diet secret?

A. I never diet. My problem is the reverse. I have to drink milk and eat sweets to keep up my weight.

Q. What personality trait would you like to change?

Q. I'm a constant worrier, and if I could, I'd change that first.

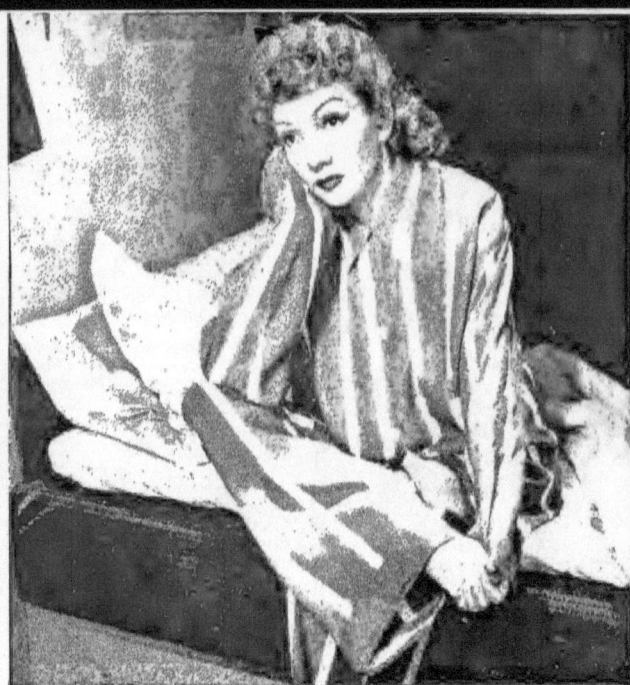

Claudette Colbert, the lovely French star, is shown in a scene from the hilarious Paramount comedy, *Palm Beach Story*, in which she co-stars with Joel McCrea

■ Cary Grant once made his living as a stilt walker. That was a long time ago —when his name was Archie Leach. Just for a laugh, comedians Bud Abbott and Lou Costello employed a stilt walker for a scene in their new picture, *It Ain't Hay*. The stilt walker carried a sign reading: "Get your clothes from Archie Leach."

■ Miriam Hopkins has moved into the beach home of Director Anatole Litvak. Litvak, who's in the Army, loaned her the house for the duration. Miriam Hopkins, incidentally, is the former Mrs. Litvak.

■ It's between scenes on the set of *The Immortal Sergeant* at 20th Century-Fox and Thomas Mitchell is in a talkative mood. "If critics never took actors apart," he says, "actors might never improve." And he cites himself as a case in point.

"I'll never forget the first time I played an Irishman. The role was nearly the ruination of what doting friends called 'a promising career.' I gave forth with a brogue that topped any I had ever heard. The critics all agreed with the one who said, 'Mr. Mitchell merits 30 lashes with a shillalah for his version of a brogue.' That did it. I made up my mind that some day producers would ask me to play accent parts."

That day has unquestionably arrived— even to Mitchell's satisfaction. In his last six pictures for 20th Century - Fox, Mitchell has spoken with five different accents—French, Scotch, Brooklyn, Cockney and Irish.

■ When Pat O'Brien signed a paper in connection with his role in *Bombardier* at R-K-O the other day, his name stretched clear across the page. It was William Joseph Patrick O'Brien. "In legal matters," the actor explained to producer Robert Fellows, "I can still keep my promise to my grandfather." It was when Pat was headed for a legal career, that he promised not to shorten his name. Even when he went on the stage, the actor tried to use his full name in billings, but it was too long. So professionally he became plain Pat O'Brien. But on legal papers, just for a proud old Irish gentleman's sake, it's William Joseph Patrick O'Brien.

■ Lon Chaney, Jr.'s make-up man on the set of *Frankenstein Meets the Wolf Man* is Max Asher, who 30 years ago was one of the top comedians of the silent films. Asher worked with the late Lon Chaney, Sr., in his first picture, a comedy, filmed by Universal in 1913. Recalls Asher: "Those were the days when Universal charged visitors 25 cents for the privilege of watching the films being made. The visitors were limited to a catwalk above the set. Your dad," he told Chaney, Jr., "used to make faces at them—and they loved him."

■ Judging by their namesakes, the most popular players in Hollywood are Tyrone Power and Sonja Henie. Madge Inman, head of the 20th Century-Fox fan mail department, reports that 571 little boys throughout the country have been

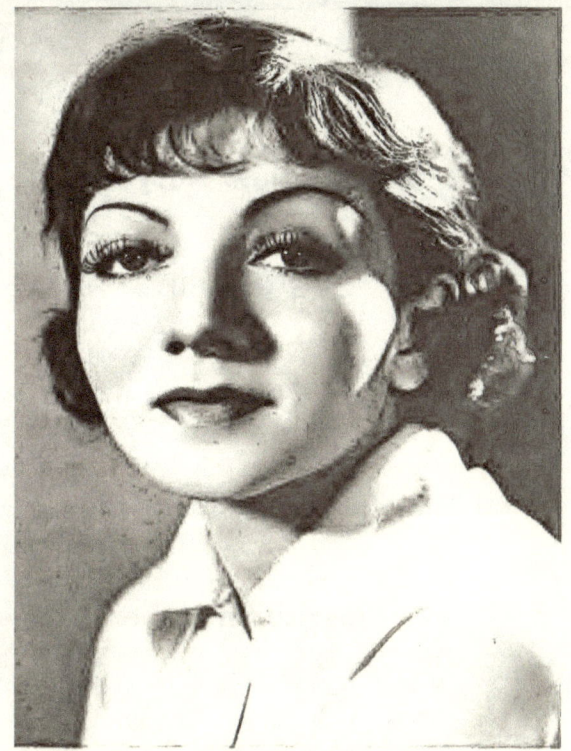

Popping Questions at Claudette Colbert

[Continued from page 31]

Q. What is your greatest fault?

A. I'm stubborn.

Q. And your greatest virtue?

A. Truthfulness.

Q. What do you think is the most unpleasant mannerism of women?

A. Coyness. I can't stand cuteness.

Q. What do you think is the most unpleasant mannerism in men?

A. Their inclination to be smug.

Q. What is the first thing you notice about a person?

A. A pleasant voice. A strident-voiced person starts out with two strikes against him, in my opinion.

Q. Who does most of the talking at home, you or your husband?

A. I do. First, because I'm more of a chatterbox than he is. Secondly, because I can talk about what's happened to me during the day—my work and activities. But my husband never discusses with me what goes on during his professional day.

Q. What feature about your face do you like the least?

A. My nose. I think it's too broad.

Q. What feature do you like the best?

A. My eyes.

Q. About what point of good grooming are you fussiest?

A. My hair. I wear it short and curled and I'm very fussy about it being just so.

Q. Do you dress to please your husband?

A. I certainly do dress to please him. He likes tailored suits, and so do I, so I didn't have to change my style for him. But he doesn't like nail polish; so my hands and toes are bare of it.

Q. Do you mind candid camera shots of yourself?

A. I hate them. I should have said that this is one of the things I don't like about my work.

Q. Have you bought any "gold bricks?"

A. Yes—my house.

Q. What unbecoming personal mannerism have you had to overcome?

A. Bad posture. I used to slump forward, and I've had to break myself of the habit.

Q. Of what personal accomplishment are you most proud?

A. Of the way I ski. I must admit I took to it very quickly and have won a few prizes.

Q. Do you believe in matrimonial vacations?

A. Definitely no. I can't see the need of them—they do more harm than good. Unfortunately, certain circumstances force separations—such as business, and now war. But I think voluntary separations are unwise.

Q. What is your favorite form of entertainment?

A. As we say in Hollywood, "Motion pictures are your best entertainment." They are for me.

Q. Who is your closest woman friend, and what qualities make her such?

A. Mrs. William Goetz, because she possesses sincerity, a great vitality, sympathy, honesty and a terrific sense of humor.

Q. Who is your closest man friend, outside of your husband?

A. My brother, Charles Wendling, and William Goetz. They both have great intelligence, a good sense of values and are most interesting conversationalists.

Q. What is your favorite color?

A. Red—on me. Blue and white—to look at.

Q. Your favorite song?

A. Cole Porter's "Night and Day."

Q. What childhood handicap or failing have you had to overcome to attain success?

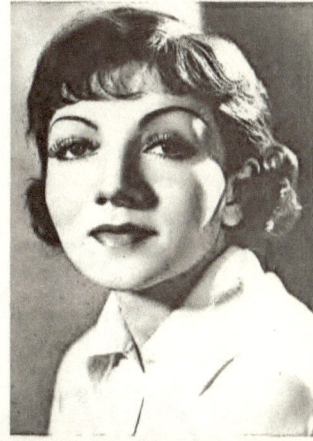

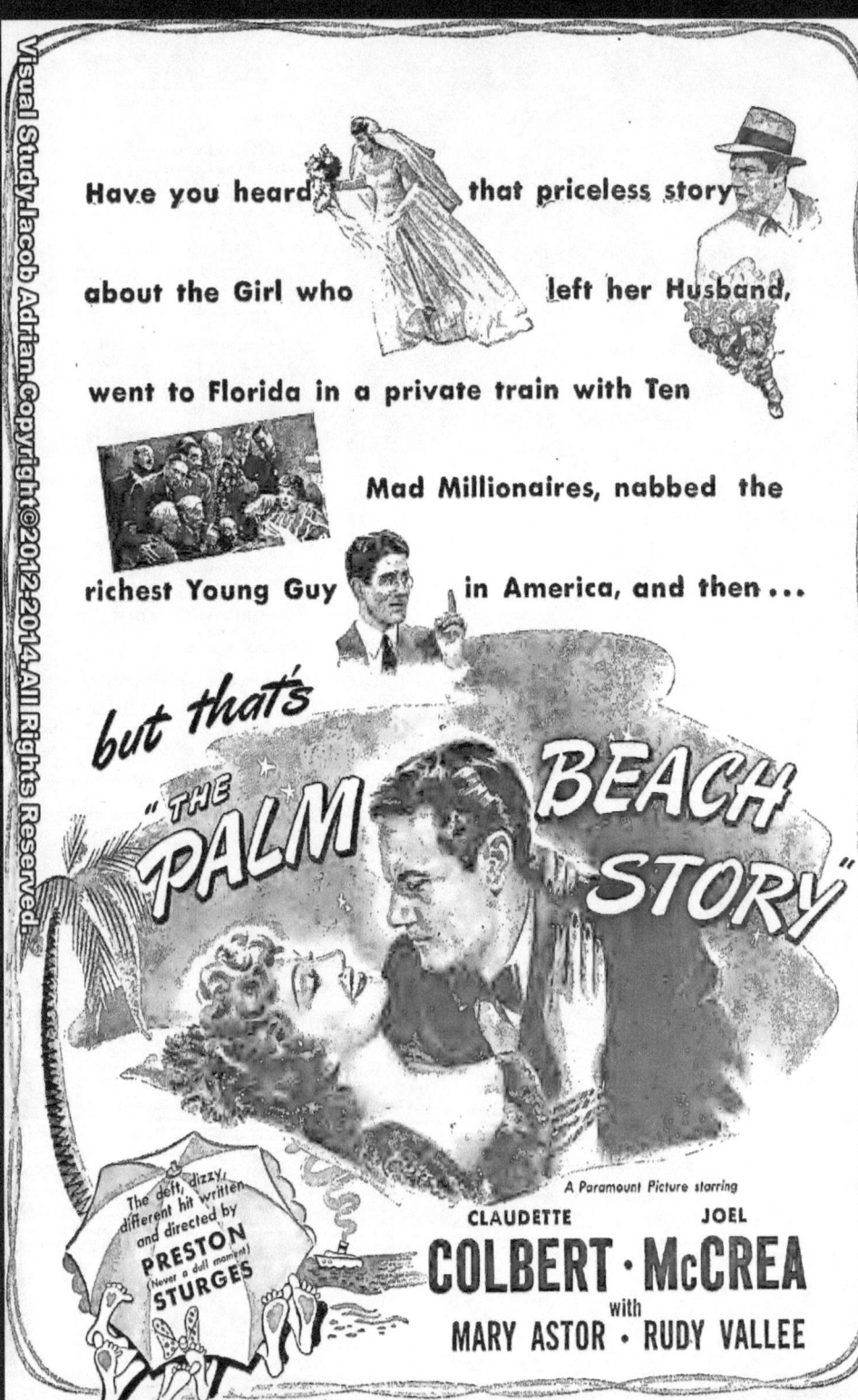

Bibliographic sources :

Hollywood (1934-1943)
Publisher: Hollywood Magazine, inc. ; Fawcett Publications, inc.

The New Movie Magazine (1929-1935)
Publisher: Tower Magazines, inc.

This documentary study use,
combined in various proportions,
elements from the following categories,
forms and subsets :
- fair use
- documentary
- documentary photography
- feature
- journalism
- arts journalism
- visual journalism
- photojournalism
- celebrity photography
in order to :
- employ material as the object of cultural critique ,
- quote to illustrate an argument or point ,
- use material in historical sequence,
providing independent opinion,
using photos, press articles, advertisements,
opinions of fans etc. ...

www.ingramcontent.com/pod-product-compliance
Lightning Source LLC
Chambersburg PA
CBHW021045180526
45163CB00005B/2299